I0416884

Table of Contents

Introduction

On September 11, 2001, Osama bin Laden and his al Qaeda network executed terrorist attacks unprecedented in scale against the United States. Prior to 9/11, such attacks generally led to robust efforts by the law enforcement community to bring the perpetrators to justice, and in limited cases, military efforts targeting those responsible. After 9/11, the Bush administration chose a bold new course, choosing to utilize military power as the primary method to pursue justice for those attacks conducted, while at the same time leveraging preemption as a means to inhibit future attacks. Also, instead of focusing his response against those responsible for 9/11, bin Laden and al Qaeda, President Bush chose to pursue a much wider, offensive campaign against terrorism and its state sponsorship. Ultimately, this broad strategy diverted manpower and resources away from the immediate threat, emboldened al Qaeda, and weakened the comprehensive national power of the United States.

This monograph will examine the threat and motivations of Osama bin Laden and al Qaeda, how these elements factored into the post-9/11 decision-making process and resultant strategy, and finally, the results and consequences of the course the United States chose to pursue in prosecuting the War on Terror. Chapter One begins with a historical review of bin Laden and al Qaeda, and demonstrates the political motivation of their campaign against America, specifically their opposition to U.S. foreign policy in the Middle East. The chapter then shows that the United States was fully aware of the threat posed by bin Laden and al Qaeda prior to 9/11, and rapidly identified them as the perpetrators within hours of the 9/11 attacks. The chapter further documents that bin Laden and al Qaeda were the sole source of international terrorism against America in the decade prior to 9/11. With this understanding, and knowing they orchestrated 9/11, the Bush administration, instead of designing a focused response targeting bin Laden and al Qaeda, chose to pursue a broad campaign against the entirety of terrorism. In addition, the administration misidentified bin Laden and al Qaeda's specific political motivations, contributing to a misguided grand strategy with long-term negative effects.

Chapter Two analyzes the planning methodology and process utilized by the Bush administration to develop the post-9/11 response. First, the decisions made in the initial days following the attacks are detailed to establish the boundaries of the nation's response. The chapter will reveal that the strategy was essentially unbounded, with no clear problem statement, and while utilizing the whole of government, depended first and foremost on military power. President Bush chose to pursue broad goals against terrorism as a whole, and its state sponsors. With broad constraints, and an unstructured planning process, the National Security Council developed a correspondingly broad and uncoordinated plan unfocused on the immediate threat, bin Laden and al Qaeda. At the same time, a parallel planning effort commenced to effect regime change in Iraq, further diverging the strategy. The chapter concludes by identifying additional factors, including the leadership style of President Bush and National Security Council shortcomings, which impacted the strategy design process.

Chapter Three documents the resultant strategy which was largely determined in the immediate hours and days after the 9/11 attacks, and was evolved and refined over the course of the next year. Following the 9/11 attacks, President Bush made a series of decisions which essentially decoupled the nation's pending response from the threat presented to it. Instead of responding against Osama bin Laden and al Qaeda, the United States would pursue a broad campaign against terrorism and its state sponsors. The chapter demonstrates how the strategy developed over the course of the next year, to include preemption as a pillar of the overarching strategy which came to be known as the 'Bush Doctrine.' The chapter concludes by highlighting actions taken across the whole of government in pursuit of the War on Terror.

The final chapter first presents a representation of alternative strategies which leveraged soft power nearly exclusively in lieu of military action. The chapter then analyzes the positive outcomes and long-term negative consequences of the War on Terror. Numerous alternative

2

strategies were available following 9/11 suggesting an array of approaches, including diplomacy, intelligence, law enforcement, and homeland security. While utilizing these areas, the Bush administration chose to focus its efforts on military power. The initial results of this strategy were positive with significant diplomatic, law enforcement, and financial achievements, as well as rapid success in the Afghanistan campaign. However, instead of consolidating and securing these gains, the Bush administration shifted its effort toward planning for and executing the war in Iraq. Consequently, the United States was drawn into fighting two prolonged conflicts over the course of the next decade. In his seminal work *Art of War*, Sun-tzu cautioned that "No country has ever profited from protracted warfare."[1] True to this advice, the United States has not profited, has not eliminated the true enemy identified on 9/11, and has instead witnessed deterioration of its comprehensive national power.

The Threat

At 9:03:11 a.m. on September 11, 2001, United Airlines Flight 175 flew into the World Trade Center's South Tower, following American Airlines Flight 11's deliberate crash into the North Tower at 8:46:40.[2] Two minutes later, at 9:05, the President's Chief of Staff approached him as he addressed an elementary school classroom in Sarasota, Florida.[3] President Bush vividly recalled the moment, "Andy Card pressed his head next to mine and whispered in my ear. 'A second plane hit the second tower,' he said, pronouncing each word deliberately in his Massachusetts accent. 'America is under attack.'"[4]

The President was soon flown to Barksdale Air Force Base, Louisiana, and then Offutt Air Force Base, Nebraska where he called a meeting of his National Security Council via secure

---

[1] Sun Tzu, *Art of War*, trans. Ralph D. Sawyer (Boulder, CO: Westview Press, 1994), 173.

[2] National Commission on Terrorist Attacks upon the United States, *The 9/11 Commission Report: Final Report of the National Commission on Terrorist Attacks upon the United States*, Washington DC, Government Printing Office, 2004, 32.

[3] Ibid., 35-38.

[4] George W. Bush, *Decision Points* (New York: Crown Publishers, 2010), 127.

3

video teleconference.[5] A mere six hours after the attacks, the scope of the American response began to take shape. President Bush opened the meeting "with a clear declaration. 'We are at war against terror.'"[6] Later that evening, he affirmed his intent to the nation during his Presidential Address from the Oval Office,[7] declaring, "America and our friends and allies join with all those who want peace and security in the world, and we stand together to win the war against terrorism."[8]

Sun-tzu's *Art of War* implores us to "know the enemy."[9] In the immediate aftermath of 9/11, did the United States clearly identify the specific threat to the nation revealed by the attacks, and then correspondingly articulate this threat in strategy development? In strategy development of any form, this clear identification and articulation of the threat is critical to defining the problem and developing appropriate courses of action. This section will begin with a historical review of Osama bin Laden and his al Qaeda network. To provide a fair assessment of the administration's actions, sources available and interviews conducted prior to 9/11 are utilized to the maximum extent possible. The section will then assess the U.S. government's identification of the threat prior to 9/11, and conclude with its subsequent assessment post-9/11.

Osama bin Laden and the al Qaeda Threat

The western perspective categorized Osama bin Laden and his al Qaeda network as terrorists. In order to fully understand bin Laden and al Qaeda, it is important to understand what terrorism is. United States Code, Title 22, Section 2656f(d) defines terrorism as "premeditated,

---

[5] According to the 9/11 Commission Report, the President arrived at Offutt Air Force Base at 2:50 p.m., and began the video teleconference at approximately 3:15.

[6] Bush, *Decision Points*, 134.

[7] Ari Fleischer, *Taking Heat: The President, the Press, and My Years in the White House* (New York: HarperCollins, 2005), 151.

[8] National Review, *"We Will Prevail": President George W. Bush on War, Terrorism, and Freedom* (New York: Continuum, 2003), 3.

[9] Sun tzu, *Art of War*, trans. Ralph D. Sawyer (Boulder, CO: Westview Press, 1994), 179.

politically motivated violence perpetrated against noncombatant targets by subnational groups or

clandestine agents."[10] Similarly, Merriam-Webster defines terrorism as "the systematic use of

terror especially as a means of coercion," with terror being defined as "violent or destructive acts

(as bombing) committed by groups in order to intimidate a population or government into

granting their demands."[11] Critical to both definitions is the aspect of political motivation. To

understand bin Laden and al Qaeda, one must understand the political motivation for their

actions. While pure hatred of the United States is commonly accepted as bin Laden's motivation,

this belief originates in his opposition to U.S. foreign policy in the Middle East.

Born in Riyadh, Saudi Arabia in 1957, Osama bin Laden was the son of Muhammed bin

Laden, a wealthy construction magnate.[12] Receiving his primary and secondary schooling in

Saudi Arabia, bin Laden formed his fundamentalist narrative at an early age. Particularly, he

adopted the beliefs espoused by the Muslim Brotherhood, whose stated goal was a return to a

singular Islamic empire. During this same timeframe, he spent his school holidays learning

construction while working with his father in the family business. Continuing his education at

King Abdul Aziz University in Jeddah, his fundamentalist views developed further as he studied

noted Islamic scholars Taqi al-Din Ibn-Tammiyah, Mohammed Qutb, and Shaykh Abdullah

Azzam, all of which preached jihad against infidels as a mechanism to protect the sanctity of

Muslim lands.[13] At the same time that bin Laden's beliefs were maturing, the Soviet Union, a

non-Muslim force, invaded Afghanistan on December 25, 1979.[14] Driven by his deep-seated

beliefs, bin Laden immediately traveled to Pakistan and Afghanistan, leveraging his construction

---

[10] U.S. Code 22, Section 2656f(d) (January 7, 2011).

[11] *Merriam-Webster Online*, s.vv. "terrorism," "terror," http://www merriam-webster.com/dictionary/terrorism (accessed December 7, 2011).

[12] Michael Scheuer, *Through Our Enemies' Eyes: Osama bin Laden, Radical Islam, and the Future of America*, Rev. ed. (Washington DC: Potomac Books, 2006), 86-88.

[13] Ibid., 92-93.

[14] John Miller, "Greetings, America. My Name is Osama bin Laden," *Esquire*, February, 1999, http://www.esquire.com/features/ESQ0299-FEB_LADEN (accessed December 8, 2011).

background and personal wealth, estimated at $250 million, to wage jihad against the infidel Soviet forces.[15]

Upon his initial arrival to the Afghanistan War, bin Laden's participation was generally limited to financial support. By 1982, he expanded his efforts, devoting substantial resources to war-focused construction projects in Afghanistan. In 1984, while continuing his construction support, he turned his focus to funding Afghan training camps, and more importantly, recruiting Arab fighters.[16] To this end, he opened Bayt al-Ansar, a receiving station, in Peshawar, Pakistan to process newly-arrived recruits for distribution to the Afghan training camps.[17] In 1986, concerned with the extensive Arab casualties caused by poor training, bin Laden began to operate his own independent Arab-only training camps. That same year, he established his base camp for Arab fighters in the Tora Bora Mountains southeast of Jalalabad.[18]

In 1988, bin Laden established an office to formalize the recording and tracking of his mujahedin fighters. The registry maintained by this office was named 'al Qaeda,' meaning 'the base' or 'foundation.'[19] It was at this time as well that bin Laden formulated his idea for an insurgent organization to survive beyond the war in Afghanistan. Bin Laden associate Abu Mahmud recalled his vision. With the emerging prospects for victory over the Soviet Union, Arab fighters were surging to Afghanistan. Bin Laden believed he could organize the Arab fighters into

---

[15] Robin Wright, "Saudi Dissident a Prime Suspect in Blasts," *Los Angeles Times*, August 14, 1998, http://articles.latimes.com/1998/aug/14/news/mn-13138 (accessed December 8, 2011).

[16] Scheuer, *Through Our Enemies' Eyes*, 103-105.

[17] Abdel Bari Atwan, *The Secret History of al Qaeda* (Berkeley, CA: University of California Press, 2006), 44.

[18] Scheuer, *Through Our Enemies' Eyes*, 108-109.

[19] Atwan, *The Secret History of al Qaeda*, 44.

an army that could answer the call for jihad in the future.[20] Islamic sources generally agree that this timeframe marked the beginning of the al Qaeda network.[21]

Bin Laden returned to Saudi Arabia after the Afghanistan war, and was soon advocating for the use of his now-idle mujahedin fighters to assist the Saudi regime. In the first of two 1990 letters to Prince Nayif bin Abdul Aziz, the Saudi Minister of the Interior, bin Laden predicted the Iraqi invasion of Kuwait. Displaying his acknowledgement of the letter's implications, the minister called a meeting with bin Laden, but took no further overt action. Following the Iraqi invasion on August 2, 1990, bin Laden sent a second letter to the minister suggesting the raising of a mujahedin army, including his veteran army from Afghanistan to defend Saudi Arabia and liberate Kuwait from the Iraqis.[22]

The Saudi regime did not accept bin Laden's offer and instead opted to host U.S. forces. During his three-day interview of bin Laden in 1996, journalist Abdel Bari Atwan recorded that,

> Bin Laden told me that the Saudi government's decision to invite US troops to defend the kingdom and liberate Kuwait was the biggest shock of his entire life. He could not believe that the House of Al Saud could welcome the deployment of 'infidel' forces on Arabian Peninsula soil, within the proximity of the Holy Places, for the first time since the inception of Islam.
> Bin Laden also feared that by welcoming US troops onto Arab land the Saudi government would be subjecting the country to foreign occupation – in an exact replay of the course of events in Afghanistan, when the Communist government in Kabul invited Russian troops into the country. Just as bin Laden had taken up arms to fight the Soviet troops in Afghanistan, he now decided to take up arms to confront the US troops on the Arabian Peninsula.[23]

Citing an obligatory fatwa issued by renowned Saudi cleric Sheikh bin Uthaymin to prepare to battle the 'invaders,' bin Laden began a mobilization effort, and took his recruits to Afghanistan, and then Sudan, where his focus was initially political activism.[24] Through the early

---

[20] Scheuer, *Through Our Enemies' Eyes*, 110.

[21] Atwan, *The Secret History of al Qaeda*, 44.

[22] Ibid., 45.

[23] Ibid., 45.

[24] Ibid., 46-48.

1990s, Muhammad Atef attested that bin Laden became unwelcome in Sudan and saw two clear choices for his future, leading to a militant mindset.[25] He could either return to Saudi Arabia, which had revoked his citizenship, and would most likely place him "under house arrest, or he could begin a full-on military campaign against his enemies, which he would continue until he was captured or killed."[26] At the same time, the influence of the radical leader of the Egyptian Islamic Jihad, Ayman al-Zawahiri, was having a profound impact on bin Laden.[27] By 1996, his strategy had shifted from activism to militarism, and he moved his operation back to Afghanistan where he would headquarter his campaign against the United States.[28]

Bin Laden wrote his initial fatwa in August, 1996. The fatwa, entitled 'Declaration of *Jihad* against the Americans Occupying the Land of the Two Sacred Places,' was initially published in the London-based Al Quds Al Arabi newspaper.[29] In October, 1996, it was further distributed via the internet.[30] This declaration against the United States largely focused on grievances related to Saudi Arabia. His argument was based on a combination of the presence of Americans on the sacred lands of Saudi Arabia, and the condition of the Saudi populace brought about by the American-supported Saudi regime. He described at length the Saudi people's "severe oppression, suffering, excessive iniquity, humiliation and poverty" as a result of their corrupt regime.[31] He then related the regime's corruption to American influence, referencing "the

---

[25] Muhammad Atef's association with bin Laden goes back to the Soviet-Afghan War where they fought together. He then followed bin Laden to Sudan and eventually rose to be Al Qaeda's Chief of Military Operations from 1996 until his death in November, 2001.

[26] Atwan, *The Secret History of al Qaeda*, 49.

[27] In 1998, al-Zawahiri merged his Egyptian Islamic Jihad group into Al Qaeda, and became the de facto second in command of Al Qaeda. Following the death of bin Laden in May, 2011, al-Zawahiri was announced as the formal leader of Al Qaeda.

[28] Atwan, *The Secret History of al Qaeda*, 49-51.

[29] Ibid., 53.

[30] Karen J. Greenberg, ed., *Al Qaeda Now: Understanding Today's Terrorists* (New York: Cambridge University Press, 2005), 159.

[31] Ibid., 162.

inability of the regime to protect the country, and allowing the enemy of the *Ummah* – the American crusader forces – to occupy the land for the longest of years. The crusader forces became the main cause of our disastrous condition."[32] For this reason, he called for the expulsion of American forces from Saudi Arabia, stating, "If there are more than one duty to be carried out, then the most important one should receive priority. Clearly after Belief (*Imaan*) there is no more important duty than pushing the American enemy out of the holy land."[33] He then succinctly summarized his political purpose and desired end state, proclaiming, "The regime is fully responsible for what had been incurred by the country and the nation; however the occupying American enemy is the principle and the main cause of the situation. Therefore efforts should be concentrated on destroying, fighting and killing the enemy until, by the Grace of Allah, it is completely defeated."[34]

During a 1997 interview with Cable News Network's Peter Arnett, and in line with his 1996 fatwa, bin Laden clarified American support of and presence in Saudi Arabia as the focal point for his campaign against the United States. When asked for his main criticism of the Saudi royal family, he stated, "The first one is their subordination to the U.S. So, our main problem is the U.S. government while the Saudi regime is but a branch or an agent of the U.S."[35] Further, when asked about continued attacks in Saudi Arabia against American military and civilians, he proclaimed, "It is known that every action has its reaction. If the American presence continues, and that is an action, then it is natural for reactions to continue against this presence."[36]

---

[32] Greenberg, *Al Qaeda Now*, 163.

[33] Ibid., 168.

[34] Ibid., 176.

[35] Osama bin Laden, interview by Peter Arnett, Afghanistan, March, 1997, transcript, http://fl1 findlaw.com/news findlaw.com/cnn/docs/binladen/binladenintvw-cnn.pdf (accessed November 25, 2011).

[36] Ibid.

While he stated that "we have focused our declaration on striking at the soldiers in the country of The Two Holy Places," the interview also eluded to an expansion of his agenda beyond Saudi Arabia.[37] Addressing Israel, he stated, "We declared jihad against the U.S. government, because the U.S. government is unjust, criminal and tyrannical. It has committed acts that are extremely unjust, hideous and criminal whether directly or through its support of the Israeli occupation of the Prophet's Night Travel Land."[38] Turning to Iraqi sanctions, he claimed, "A reaction might take place as a result of U.S. government's hitting Muslim civilians and executing more than 600 thousand Muslim children in Iraq by preventing food and medicine from reaching them."[39] Finally, summarizing a set of grievances broader than just American presence in Saudi Arabia, he proclaimed, "The driving-away jihad against the U.S. does not stop with its withdrawal from the Arabian peninsula, but rather it must desist from aggressive intervention against Muslims in the whole world."[40]

During the same timeframe, July, 1996, and March, 1997, bin Laden concluded a series of three interviews with decorated British foreign correspondent Robert Fisk, dictating parallel sentiments.[41] Similar to the Arnett interview, bin Laden's hatred centered on his views toward a corrupt Saudi regime, its American support, and American presence following the Iraqi invasion of Kuwait. He pointed to the "big mistake by the Saudi regime of inviting the American troops," and claimed, "The solution to this crisis is the withdrawal of American troops... their military presence is an insult to the Saudi people."[42] Further analogous to the Arnett interview with

---

[37] Osama bin Laden, interview by Peter Arnett.

[38] Ibid.

[39] Ibid.

[40] Ibid.

[41] Robert Fisk's first interview with Osama bin Laden took place in Sudan in 1993.

[42] Robert Fisk, "Osama bin Laden: The Godfather of Terror," *The Independent*, September 15, 2001, http://www.independent.co.uk/news/people/profiles/osama-bin-laden-the-godfather-of-terror-751944.html (accessed August 25, 2011).

respect to Israel and Iraqi sanctions, Fisk relayed that "there was no difference, he said, between the American and Israeli governments, between the American and Israeli armies."[43] Bin Laden then related that "killing those Iraqi children is a crusade against Islam. We, as Muslims, do not like the Iraqi regime but we think that the Iraqi people and their children are our brothers and we care about their future."[44]

On February 23, 1998, bin Laden merged al-Zawahiri's Egyptian Islamic Jihad under the al Qaeda umbrella, creating the World Islamic Front for Jihad against the Jews and Crusaders.[45] To announce the unification, bin Laden, al-Zawahiri, and several other extremist leaders co-signed what is regarded as bin Laden's second fatwa against America. The statement clearly articulated three specific grievances. First was the seven-year occupation of the lands of Islam by the United States. Second was the devastation inflicted on the Iraqi people by sanctions against their regime, and potential further American aggression against Iraq. Third was the American alliance with Israel.[46] The following fatwa was then issued, "The ruling to kill the Americans and their allies—civilians and military—is an individual duty for every Muslim who can do it in any country in which it is possible to do it, in order to liberate the al-Aqsa Mosque and the holy mosque from their grip, and in order for their armies to move out of all the lands of Islam, defeated and unable to threaten any Muslim."[47] The fatwa made clear that bin Laden's motivation was American presence and policy toward the Middle East.

Bin Laden continued his consistent messaging during two 1998 interviews, the first with American Broadcasting Company's John Miller in May, 1998. During this interview, he stated, "The call to wage war against America was made because America has spear-headed the crusade

---

[43] Fisk, "Osama bin Laden: The Godfather of Terror".

[44] Ibid.

[45] Atwan, *The Secret History of al Qaeda*, 79.

[46] Osama bin Laden, "Second Fatwa" (published in Al Quds Al Arabi, London, February 23, 1998).

[47] Ibid.

11

against the Islamic nation, sending tens of thousands of its troops to the land of the two Holy

Mosques over and above its meddling in its affairs and its politics, and its support of the

oppressive, corrupt and tyrannical regime that is in control. These are the reasons behind the

singling out of America as a target."[48] He further vowed "to fight until the Americans are driven

out of all the Islamic countries."[49] Putting action to words, al Qaeda executed the East African

embassy bombings in Kenya and Tanzania in August, 1998, to which the United States responded

with cruise missile strikes against suspected al Qaeda targets in Afghanistan and Sudan. Bin

Laden then reinforced his message during his December, 1998 interview with al-Jazeera. When

asked what he sought, he answered, "We demand that our land be liberated from enemies. That

our lands be liberated from the Americans."[50] When asked what his end objectives were, he

answered, "So this is our aim – to liberate the lands of Islam from the sinners."[51]

   After moving back to Afghanistan in 1996, bin Laden was clear and consistent in

articulating his political aims. Beginning with opposition to American military presence in Saudi

Arabia, and expanding to the impact of Iraqi sanctions and support for Israel, the common theme

of his grievances was American presence in and policy toward the Middle East. Bin Laden made

multiple proclamations via his fatwas, and initiated numerous interviews with western journalists

to carry his message. Journalist Peter Bergen, while discussing bin Laden's motivations,

emphatically stated, "What he condemns the United States for is simple: its policies in the Middle

East."[52] He continued, "Bin Laden is at war with the United States, but his is a political war."[53]

---

[48] Osama bin Laden, interview by John Miller, Afghanistan, May 28, 1998, transcript, http://www.pbs.org/wgbh/pages/frontline/shows/binladen/who/interview.html (accessed August 25, 2011).

[49] Ibid.

[50] Osama bin Laden, interview by al-Jazeera, Afghanistan, December, 1998, transcript, http://www.freerepublic.com/focus/f-news/542192/posts (accessed August 25, 2011).

[51] Ibid.

[52] Peter L. Bergen, *Holy War, Inc.: Inside the Secret World of Osama bin Laden* (New York: Simon & Schuster, 2002), 227.

[53] Ibid., 227.

Prior to 9/11, the threat, and corresponding political motivation, posed by Osama bin Laden and al Qaeda were clear.

U.S. Government pre-9/11 Identification of the Threat

Prior to 9/11, the nature of the threat posed by bin Laden and al Qaeda was known by the U.S. government. While, arguably, the imminence of the threat was not appreciated or acted upon, it nevertheless was known. The government's three lead agencies for combating terrorism, the Central Intelligence Agency (CIA), Federal Bureau of Investigation (FBI), and Department of State, were all aware of, and tracking, bin Laden and al Qaeda. In addition to acknowledgement of the threat, the government, through its own investigations and indictments, knew that every major external terrorist attack against the United States in the decade prior to 9/11 could be traced to bin Laden and al Qaeda. Finally, both President Clinton and President Bush, as well as their administrations, had intimate knowledge of the threat posed by bin Laden and al Qaeda.

Within the CIA, analyst Gina Bennett provided the first warning of Osama bin Laden and al Qaeda in 1993. Her recently declassified background paper for the Department of State's Bureau of Intelligence and Research described bin Laden, living at the time in Khartoum, Sudan, as a religious zealot and financier of "Islamic militants operating in places as diverse as Yemen and the U.S."[54] While not using the term al Qaeda, the paper documented the potential for terrorist operations emanating from the residual pool of Arab fighter remaining after the Soviet-Afghan War. She ominously described their logistics, communications, and technical skills, as well as ready access to financing.[55]

---

[54] Gina Bennett, *The Wandering Mujahidin: Armed and Dangerous* (Washington DC: U.S. Department of State Bureau of Intelligence and Research, August 21-22, 1993), 2, http://www.nationalsecuritymom.com/3/WanderingMujahidin.pdf (accessed December 9, 2011).

[55] Ibid., 2.

In 1996, the CIA established an experimental stateside unit titled 'Terrorist Financial Links,' which quickly became more focused and morphed to the 'Bin Laden Issue Station.' The unit ultimately operated for nearly ten years.[56] For the next five years leading to 9/11, the CIA used National Intelligence Estimates, Presidential Daily Briefs, Congressional testimony, and personal letters from the Director to the President to warn of the threat posed by bin Laden and al Qaeda. Bin Laden's network and Afghanistan became the focal point for CIA collection efforts. Satellites were repositioned, human sources were cultivated, and Predator drones began collecting over Afghanistan.[57] Finally, the CIA was granted Presidential covert action authority to plan capture operations against bin Laden.[58] From CIA Director George Tenet's perspective, there was no doubt that both the Clinton and Bush administrations understood the magnitude of the threat. He argued, "The 9/11 Commission suggested that in the run-up to 9/11 policy makers across two administrations did not fully understand the magnitude of the terrorist threat. This is nonsense."[59]

Similar efforts began in December, 1995 at the FBI, where Special Agent Daniel Coleman opened the Bureau's first counterterrorism case against bin Laden.[60] He was then detailed to the CIA in 1996 specifically to investigate bin Laden.[61] Following the al Qaeda terrorist attacks of the 1990s, and the multiple corresponding indictments against bin Laden, he entered the FBI's 'Ten Most Wanted Fugitive List' in June 1999.[62]

---

[56] George Tenet, *At the Center of the Storm: My Years at the CIA* (New York: HarperCollins, 2007), 100-101.

[57] Ibid., 120-127.

[58] Ibid., 109.

[59] Ibid., 129-130.

[60] Peter L. Bergen, *The Longest War: The Enduring Conflict Between America and Al-Qaeda* (New York: Free Press, 2011), 38.

[61] Benjamin Weiser, "Prosecutors are Expected to Seek Dismissal of Charges Against Bin Laden," *New York Times*, May 3, 2011, http://www.nytimes.com/2011/05/04/nyregion/with-bin-ladens-death-seeking-the-dismissal-of-all-charges.html (accessed December 10, 2011).

[62] FBI, FBI Ten Most Wanted Fugitive List, http://www.fbi.gov/wanted/topten/usama-bin-laden (accessed November 20, 2011).

Consistent with the CIA and FBI, the Department of State recognized the danger posed by bin Laden and the al Qaeda network prior to 9/11. Their annual *Patterns of Global Terrorism* publication provided specific warning of bin Laden and al Qaeda as early as the 1998 edition. Each edition detailed bin Laden's stated political goals, public threats against America, and al Qaeda network, as well as their training and safe haven in Afghanistan.[63]

In addition to awareness of the threat by the nation's top three counterterrorist organizations, there was a clear pattern of culpability in terrorist acts toward the United States in the 1990s, all acknowledged and documented by the U.S. government. Prior to the 1990s, terrorist attacks against the United States were largely traceable to either American participation in Lebanese peacekeeping operations or to Libyan origins. This pattern shifted to bin Laden and al Qaeda in the decade prior to 9/11.

The emergent pattern of the 1990s began in 1992 with the attempted bombing of American Soldiers transiting Aden, Yemen for Somalia. The Department of State's *Patterns of Global Terrorism 2000* stated that al Qaeda claimed responsibility for the bombings.[64] Bin Laden was later indicted in June, 1998 by a U.S. Federal Grand Jury in New York for plotting the attack, the first of a series of indictments against him.[65] A superseding November, 1998 indictment added charges related to the October 3-4, 1993 killing of eighteen U.S. Army personnel in Somalia, and the August 7, 1998 bombings of the U.S. Embassies in Kenya and Tanzania.[66] Demonstrating further terrorist attack links to bin Laden and al Qaeda, the 1999 attack on the

---

[63] U.S. Department of State, *Patterns of Global Terrorism* (Washington DC, 1998-2000).

[64] U.S. Department of State, *Patterns of Global Terrorism* (Washington DC, 2000), 69.

[65] Tenet, *At the Center of the Storm*, 108-109.

[66] United States v. Usama bin Laden, S(2) 98 Cr. 1023 (LBS) (S. district of N.Y. 1998).

U.S.S. Cole was alleged via federal indictment to be planned by bin Laden and executed by al Qaeda associates.[67]

Of the four remaining significant terrorist attacks against the United States in the 1990s, three presented suspect, but not concrete, evidence of bin Laden and al Qaeda involvement. Ramzi Yousef, nephew of eventual al Qaeda operations chief Khalid Shaykh Mohammed,[68] masterminded the 1993 World Trade Center Bombing and was reported by Pakistani investigators to the CIA to have been harbored at a bin Laden guesthouse in Pakistan's Peshawar province for up to three years prior to his arrest in 1995.[69] Turning to the 1995 and 1996 attacks in Riyadh and Dhahran, Saudi Arabia, the *9/11 Commission Report*, using pre-9/11 sources, claimed that bin Laden associates took credit for the Riyadh attack, and acknowledged "signs that al Qaeda played some role" in Dhahran's Khobar Towers attack.[70] In interviews following these attacks, bin Laden claimed to Miller to have "instigated" the attacks,[71] and to Atwan that al Qaeda was behind the Khobar Towers attacks, and had follow-on attacks planned until the U.S. relocated its forces to al-Kharj, a military base south of Riyadh.[72] With the exception of the Oklahoma City bombing in 1995, every major terrorist attack against the United States in the decade leading to 9/11 could be traced to some degree, whether perceived or real, to Osama bin Laden and al Qaeda.

President Clinton unquestionably understood the danger of bin Laden and al Qaeda, naming him "public enemy number one."[73] Witnessing the series of al Qaeda-related terrorist

---

[67] John Ashcroft, Remarks of Attorney General John Ashcroft: Indictment for the Bombing of the U.S.S. Cole, Washington, DC, May 15, 2003.

[68] Scheuer, *Through Our Enemies' Eyes*, 246.

[69] CIA, *Usama bin Laden: Islamic Extremist Financier* (Washington DC, 1996).

[70] *The 9/11 Commission Report*, 60.

[71] Osama bin Laden, interview by John Miller.

[72] Atwan, *The Secret History of al Qaeda*, 36.

[73] Huma Khan, "Osama Bin Laden Dead, But Costly War on Terror Goes On," ABC News, May 3, 2011, http://abcnews.go.com/Politics/osama-bin-laden-dead-alleged-911-planners-death/story?id=13511388 (accessed December 11, 2011).

attacks during his presidency, he signed a series of Memorandums of Notification for the CIA to oversee capture, and later kill, covert operations against bin Laden.[74] On August, 20, 1998 he authorized retaliatory cruise missile strikes against bin Laden and al Qaeda for their Embassy bombings in Kenya and Tanzania. On the same day, he instituted financial sanctions against bin Laden and al Qaeda by signing Executive Order 13099.[75] Finally, in his August 20, 1998 Presidential Address announcing retaliatory strikes, President Clinton described bin Laden as "perhaps the preeminent organizer and financier of international terrorism in the world today."[76]

The Bush administration also understood the imminent danger. Following the inauguration in January, 2001, the new administration was quickly made aware of the growing al Qaeda threat. On January 25, 2001, Richard Clarke, the head of the administration's Counterterrorism Security Group, sent a memorandum to the new National Security Advisor, Condoleezza Rice, requesting an urgent Principal's review to discuss counterterrorism policy with regards to al Qaeda.[77] He also personally briefed Rice, as well as her deputy, Stephen Hadley, Vice President Dick Cheney, and Secretary of State Colin Powell on the al Qaeda threat and the necessity to assume an offensive mindset.[78] Acting slowly, but nonetheless acknowledging the issue, the Deputies Committee met on March 7, 2001, and then again on April 30, 2001 to discuss policy regarding al Qaeda.[79] Questioned about the emphasis on al Qaeda and bin Laden as the threat, Clarke set the tone for the discussion, "We are talking about that network

---

[74] *The 9/11 Commission Report*, 126, 132.

[75] Executive Order no. 13099, *Code of Federal Regulations*, title 3, p. 208 (1998).

[76] William J. Clinton, Presidential Address, Washington DC, August 20, 1998, http://www.pbs.org/newshour/bb/military/july-dec98/clinton2_8-20.html (accessed December 11, 2011).

[77] *The 9/11 Commission Report*, 201.

[78] Richard A. Clarke, *Against All Enemies: Inside America's War on Terror* (New York: Free Press, 2004), 227.

[79] *The 9/11 Commission Report*, 203.

because it and it alone poses an immediate and serious threat to the United States."[80] As a result of these meetings, a National Security Presidential Directive was drafted which was eventually discussed during a September 4, 2011 Principals Committee meeting. Following the meeting, Rice requested the directive be finalized for the President's signature.[81]

At the same time the National Security Council was considering policy options, the CIA continued its persistence in warning of an imminent attack. On July 10, 2001, witnessing a crescendo of al Qaeda-related threat reporting, Director Tenet called an urgent meeting with Rice. The opening line of the presentation set the tone, "There will be a significant terrorist attack in the coming weeks or months."[82] The briefing detailed emerging bin Laden and al Qaeda intelligence, and argued for offensive actions to counter the pending threat.[83] The CIA warned the President directly as well. When specifically asked by the President if intelligence indicated an attack inside the United States by al Qaeda, the August 6, 2001 Presidential daily briefing was drafted.[84] It warned that "clandestine, foreign government, and media reports indicate bin Laden since 1997 has wanted to conduct terrorist attacks in the U.S."[85] The brief detailed that, according to a classified source, "After U.S. missile strikes on his base in Afghanistan in 1998, bin Laden told followers he wanted to retaliate in Washington."[86] It then provided more specific, though uncorroborated, warning related to aircraft hijackings. The report stated that "bin Laden wanted

---

[80] Clarke, *Against All Enemies*, 231.

[81] Ibid., 238.

[82] Tenet, *At the Center of the Storm*, 108-109.

[83] Ibid., 151-153.

[84] Ibid., 158-159.

[85] President's Daily Brief, August 6, 2001, The Osama bin Laden File, National Security Archive Electronic Briefing Book No. 343, http://www.gwu.edu/~nsarchiv/NSAEBB/NSAEBB343/osama_bin_laden_file02.pdf (accessed November 26, 2011).

[86] Ibid.

to hijack a U.S. aircraft," and that "FBI information since that time indicates patterns of suspicious activity in this country consistent with preparations for hijackings."[87]

Undoubtedly, the U.S. government was aware of the threat, capability and intent of bin Laden and al Qaeda prior to 9/11. The CIA, FBI, and Department of State had identified bin Laden as a preeminent terrorist and financier since the early 1990s. Based on the reality of terrorist attacks of the 1990s, al Qaeda was the primary terrorist threat to the nation. Finally, the awareness of the threat went to the top levels of government. Both the Clinton and Bush administrations acknowledged the danger of Osama bin Laden and al Qaeda.

U.S. Government post-9/11 Identification of the Threat

Bin Laden and al Qaeda were rapidly identified as being responsible for the terrorist attacks of 9/11; however, the nature of the conflict quickly expanded to include much broader aims, to include state actors. In addition, bin Laden's motivation, or 'why,' was not correctly established. Specific evidence pointed to al Qaeda within hours of the attack. While acknowledging al Qaeda as the perpetrator of the attacks, President Bush immediately expanded his focus well beyond just al Qaeda. Also, despite clear evidence implicating al Qaeda, members of the administration immediately began to seek culpability of state sponsors beyond Afghanistan. Further, despite years of clear articulation of bin Laden's motivation, the administration failed to recognize that the attacks were related to American foreign policy.

On 9/11, following the attacks, the CIA's Counterterrorism Center requested, received, and analyzed the hijacked planes passenger manifests. The names of suspected al Qaeda members were immediately identified. Director Tenet stated, "That was the first time we had absolute proof of what I had been virtually certain of from the moment I heard about the attacks: we were in the

---

[87] President's Daily Brief, August 6, 2001.

19

middle of an al-Qa'ida plot."[88] When asked by the Vice President, then later by President Bush during his National Security Council secure video teleconference, who was responsible for the attacks, Director Tenet confidently answered "al-Qa'ida."[89] In his memoirs, President Bush recounted that "by the afternoon of 9/11, the intelligence community had discovered known Al Qaeda operatives on the passenger manifests of the hijacked planes."[90] He further acknowledged that on September 12, 2001, "George Tenet confirmed that bin Laden was responsible for the attacks. Intelligence intercepts had revealed al Qaeda members congratulating one another in eastern Afghanistan."[91] On the day of the attacks, and without question by the next day, the administration knew that Osama bin Laden and al Qaeda were responsible.

As quickly as the administration was identifying the perpetrators of the 9/11 attacks, President Bush was formulating his expanded notion of the enemy. Discussing his first meeting of the National Security Council after the attacks, via video teleconference from Offutt Air Force Base, he recounted, "I had thought carefully about what I wanted to say. I started with a clear declaration. 'We are at war against terror.'"[92] Independent of this announcement, a similar conclusion was reached by a group of senior civilian and military officials returning to the United States from Europe on a KC-135 tanker the next day. During their impromptu strategy planning session, led by Douglas Feith, the Under Secretary of Defense for Policy, they agreed that while speculation focused on al Qaeda, "We did not yet know who did it. In our airplane discussions, we recognized that identifying the perpetrators was not the same as deciding how to define the

---

[88] Tenet, *At the Center of the Storm*, 167.

[89] Ibid., 169.

[90] Bush, *Decision Points*, 134.

[91] Ibid., 141.

[92] Ibid., 134.

enemy. If the proper top priority of U.S. action was to prevent the next attack, after all, then the enemy was not just the particular group responsible for the 9/11 hijackings."[93]

This dichotomy was articulated by President Bush to the nation on September 20, 2001, during his Presidential Address to Congress. During the address, he clearly defined who executed the attacks, "The evidence we have gathered all points to a collection of loosely affiliated terrorist organizations known as al Qaeda." He then named bin Laden as al Qaeda's leader.[94] However, he subsequently expanded his notion of the enemy by stating, "Our war on terror begins with al Qaeda, but it does not end there. It will not end until every terrorist group of global reach has been found, stopped and defeated."[95]

Related to the immediate expansion of the threat, there was a corresponding effort to assign responsibility to state sponsorship outside of Afghanistan, namely Iraq. Director Tenet recalled passing Richard Perle, the head of the Secretary of Defense's Defense Policy Board, as he entered the White House on September 12. Perle was matter of fact in stating, "Iraq has to pay a price for what happened yesterday. They bear responsibility."[96] Clarke recollected similar sentiments in discussions at the White House the same day concerning Iraq as a target. He recalled Deputy Secretary of Defense Paul Wolfowitz being convinced that al Qaeda was incapable of executing the 9/11 attacks alone. His belief was that they were aided by a state supporter, namely Iraq. Similarly, Secretary of Defense Rumsfeld was lobbying for a broad set of objectives in response to 9/11, to include "getting Iraq."[97]

Akin to expanding the notion of the threat beyond the actual perpetrators of the attacks, the administration had similar difficulty ascribing the reasons for the attacks. Representative of al

---

[93] Douglas Feith, *War and Decision: Inside the Pentagon at the Dawn of the War on Terrorism* (New York: HarperCollins, 2008), 6.

[94] National Review, *"We Will Prevail"*, 12-13.

[95] Ibid., 14.

[96] Tenet, *At the Center of the Storm*, xix.

[97] Clarke, *Against All Enemies*, 30.

Qaeda assessments accomplished prior to 9/11, Sandia National Laboratories captured the essence of bin Laden's grievances. Their 1999 case study found that the goals of al Qaeda included withdrawal of American forces from Saudi Arabia, reduction of global American influence in the Islamic world, overthrow of secular regimes in Arab world, largely supported by the United States, and establishment of Islamic states or a larger Caliphate.[98]

To answer the 'why' question, the President evolved from an ideological explanation to a politically-motivated rationale. However, largely ignoring bin Laden's consistent narrative, President Bush failed to identify American foreign policy and presence in the Middle East as the motivating factor. Beginning with a purely ideological basis during his Address to the Nation the evening of the attacks, the President stated, "America was targeted for attack because we're the brightest beacon for freedom and opportunity in the world."[99] Later, during his September 20 Address to Congress, he answered the "why do they hate us" question with a combination of ideological and political reasons, while avoiding any attribution to U.S. foreign policy in the Middle East, as consistently documented by bin Laden's numerous interviews, fatwas and speeches.[100] Finally, during his speech to the United Nations General Assembly on November 10, 2001, President Bush proclaimed, "They kill because they aspire to dominate. They seek to overthrow governments and destabilize entire regions."[101]

Within the administration, there was a similar failure to accurately identify bin Laden's motivation. Presidential speechwriter David Frum observed two camps form in the White House regarding the 'why do they hate us' question. The first camp, led by Karen Hughes, focused on the belief that the Muslim world did not understand the United States. Correspondingly, her camp

---

[98] Sandia National Laboratories, *Osama bin Laden: A Case Study* (Livermore, CA, December 1999), 15, http://www.gwu.edu/~nsarchiv/NSAEBB/NSAEBB343/osama_bin_laden_file04.pdf (accessed December 5, 2011).

[99] National Review, *"We Will Prevail"*, 2.

[100] Ibid., 14.

[101] Ibid., 68.

argued for a robust public diplomacy campaign. The second camp, led by Karl Rove, believed the root cause was the Muslim world's resentment of U.S. power. He argued for enforced respect.[102] Secretary Rumsfeld's argument encapsulated the administration's inability to offer an accurate explanation for the 9/11 attacks. In his memoirs, he argued, "The war declared on us was not about any particular policy dispute."[103] He then specifically dismissed bin Laden's grievances of American presence in Saudi Arabia and Israeli policy, and offered the Islamic extremists' desire for an overarching caliphate as the solitary reason for the attacks.[104]

In the immediate aftermath of the attacks, the President and his administration had difficulty maintaining focus on the proven perpetrators, and instead rapidly crafted arguments for an expansion to the whole of terrorism, and state sponsorship. They struggled equally to explain the political motivations for the attacks. Summarizing these shortfalls, Frum explained his observations of the administration's reaction to the attacks, "In 2001, nothing seemed clear: not the identity of America's enemy, not the nature of the conflict, not the definition of victory."[105]

Strategy Design Methodology

In the days and weeks following the 9/11 attacks, the lack of focus and understanding by the administration on Osama bin Laden, al Qaeda, and their motivations carried forward to influence the subsequent strategy design process. Without clear focus on a specific adversary, the development of an appropriate strategy was correspondingly imprecise and rapidly diverged, thus diluting its overall effectiveness. Emphasizing the necessity of focus, former CIA Counterterrorism Center Chief Vincent Cannistraro testified before the House International Relations Committee on October 3, 2001, "They (terrorist organizations and state sponsors

---

[102] David Frum, *The Right Man: The Surprise Presidency of George W. Bush* (New York: Random House, 2003), 170.

[103] Donald Rumsfeld, *Known and Unknown: A Memoir* (New York: Sentinel, 2011), 354.

[104] Ibid., 354.

[105] Frum, *The Right Man*, 141.

beyond al Qaeda and the Taliban) were not involved with this operation. We have to focus on the immediate objective, which is the nerve center in Afghanistan and its connections around the world. The problem is if we lose our focus, we will not be able to root out this evil."[106] He then stressed, "We need a better focus on understanding what the nature of this threat is if we are to have any success in defeating it."[107] By expanding the threat beyond bin Laden and al Qaeda, and further not appreciating their motivations, President Bush did not understand the nature of the threat, thus introducing confusion and distraction into the national security planning team's deliberations.

This section will examine the post-9/11 strategy development methodology of the administration. First, the section will expand upon the President's immediate notion that the nation's response would target terrorism as a whole versus the specific perpetrators of 9/11. In not accurately defining the problem, the administration rapidly diverged, versus being focused, in strategy development. The section will then analyze the strategy design process that occurred in the first week after the attacks, and document the divergent Iraq planning effort. Finally the section will offer additional negative factors inhibiting the post-9/11 policymaking process.

Expansion of the Threat

Central to any problem-solving approach is to accurately identify the problem. Representative of this notion, the Department of Defense's planning doctrine states that, "Defining the problem is essential to solving the problem. It involves understanding and isolating the root causes of the issue at hand—defining the essence of a complex, ill-defined problem."[108] The boundaries that would shape strategy in response to the 9/11 attacks were dictated within

---

[106] House Committee on International Relations, *Hearing on al Qaeda and the Global Reach of Terrorism*, 107th Cong., 1st sess., October 3, 2001.

[107] Ibid.

[108] U.S. Department of Defense, *Joint Publication 5-0: Joint Operation Planning* (Washington DC, August 11,2011), xx-xxi.

forty-eight hours of the attacks. Instead of a focused response against bin Laden and al Qaeda, the President chose to pursue a broad campaign against both terrorists and their sponsors to eradicate the whole of terrorism. As a result, the administration was virtually unbound in its consideration of potential strategies. By immediately broadening the conflict beyond bin Laden and al Qaeda, and not accurately answering the 'why' question in relation to the attacks, the administration set the stage toward developing a strategy in absence of a clear articulation of the problem.

The broad constraints on America's response were set decisively by President Bush nearly immediately after the attacks without hearing or considering advice from his national security team. Confirming his resolve from the previous day's National Security Council video teleconference, the President declared to Congressional leaders on September 12, "We're fighting terrorism, not a cell."[109] Expanding from this mindset, he made two additional decisions that would frame the conflict from the outset. First was the decision that it would be a war. The second was to hold both the terrorists, and their state sponsors responsible.[110] Frum recounted that the President made these decisions within hours of the attacks. The President confirmed these decisions at his September 12 National Security Council meeting, stressing his intent to go after not only those responsible for 9/11, but terrorists in general and states that harbored them.[111]

On September 15, the President publicly summarized the pending campaign in his Radio Address to the Nation, stating, "Victory against terrorism will not take place in a single battle, but in a series of decisive actions against terrorist organizations and those who harbor and support them. We are planning a broad and sustained campaign to secure our country and eradicate the evil of terrorism."[112] Frum described a fundamental shift represented by the President's early decision-making, stating that he effectively "discarded thirty-five years of American policy in the

---

[109] Fleischer, *Taking Heat*, 157.

[110] Frum, *The Right Man*, 141-142.

[111] Tenet, *At the Center of the Storm*, 175.

[112] National Review, *"We Will Prevail"*, 8.

Middle East and repudiated the foreign policies of at least six of the previous seven U.S. presidents."[113] With the exception of the 1986 bombing of Libya, the United States had previously depended on a combination of law enforcement, covert action, and diplomacy to combat terrorism.[114] For this war, President Bush made clear that any and all resources available to the nation, to include the military, would be leveraged.

The President's broad and unfocused approach quickly manifested itself in the planning deliberations of the administration. Clarke witnessed White House discussions on September 12 and 13 revolving around who the enemy was and what the scope of the response would be. The consensus was that the response would begin in Afghanistan against al Qaeda and the Taliban, but that would only be the first step in a broader campaign.[115] Similar conclusions were being reached by Under Secretary Feith and his impromptu planning team. During their return from Europe on September 12, they discussed a preventative strategy that "recognized that the enemy was a wide-ranging set of individuals, organizations, and states."[116] Finally, the President himself began to insinuate divergent strategy away from bin Laden and al Qaeda. On the evening of September 12, at the White House, Clarke recalled the following exchange with President Bush, "'See if Saddam did this. See if he's linked in any way...' I was once again taken aback, incredulous, and it showed. 'But, Mr. President, al Qaeda did this.' 'I know, I know, but... see if Saddam was involved. Just look. I want to know any shred.'"[117] Within two days of the attacks, the President had set the stage for a nearly unbounded strategy design process, diluting the focus on the actual enemy, bin Laden and al Qaeda.

---

[113] Frum, *The Right Man*, 142.

[114] Ibid., 143.

[115] Clarke, *Against All Enemies*, 31.

[116] Feith, *War and Decision*, 6.

[117] Clarke, *Against All Enemies*, 32.

Rapid Evolution from Attack to Action

Rather than a regulated methodology informed by a specific problem statement and driven by focused goals, the strategy design process was limited to a short series of unstructured National Security Council meetings, discussions and debates. The methodology was not informed by a holistic analysis of the situation, answering the fundamental questions of who attacked the United States and why. In military planning, problem identification informs a 'mission analysis,' which leads to formulation of appropriate courses of action for comparison and selection. Department of Defense Joint Doctrine emphasizes that, "Mission analysis is critical because it provides direction to the commander and the staff, enabling them to focus effectively on the problem at hand."[118] The available literature describing the post-9/11 strategy formulation indicates that a robust 'mission analysis' did not take place. As a result, the planning process began at the course of action development stage in the absence of an accurate and focused problem to solve. Further, the lack of focus allowed the administration to rapidly diverge toward policy goals, such as Iraq regime change, that were unrelated to the immediate problem, Osama bin Laden and his al Qaeda network.

Instigated by President Bush's pronouncement of a war against the whole of terrorism, the Cabinet departments aggressively devised actions within their scopes of responsibility. These plans were briefed to the President during National Security Council meetings on September 13 and 14, 2001. Focused in their argument, the Department of State advocated for a narrow approach concentrated on al Qaeda. Incorporating a longer term perspective, and consideration of terrorist motivations, Secretary Powell briefed international offers of assistance and cooperation, and identified the need to jumpstart Arab-Israeli diplomacy.[119] Looking toward a battle of ideas, Secretary Powell's talking points for the September 14, 2001 Principals meeting stated, "My

---

[118] *Joint Publication 5-0*, xxvi.

[119] Feith, *War and Decision*, 13.

27

sense is that moderate Arabs are starting to see terrorism in a whole new light. This is key to the coalition."[120] The Department of State's overarching 'Action Plan' included far-ranging diplomatic efforts to harness international condemnation and assistance in response to 9/11. The plan included completed and planned diplomatic efforts with the United Nations, North Atlantic Treaty Organization, European Union, and the Group of Eight, as well as engagements with countries ranging from Iran, India, Pakistan, and Sudan, to Russia, its former Central Asian republics, China, and Indonesia.[121]

The Departments of Justice, Treasury, Defense, and the CIA were equally aggressive in their domains. The Department of Justice, leveraging the Immigration and Naturalization Service and FBI, immediately began to arrest individuals with immigration violations and links to the 9/11 attacks. At the same time, they began to shift from a prosecutorial to a preventative mindset.[122] Secretary of the Treasury O'Neill briefed the legal status of his Department's actions to target terrorist financing.[123] Within the Department of Defense, Chairman of the Joint Chiefs of Staff, General Hugh Shelton directed United States Central Command to develop military options for action against Afghanistan.[124] Finally, the CIA, drawing on their previous planning efforts, briefed the War Cabinet on their proposal to defeat both al Qaeda and the Taliban in Afghanistan using paramilitary teams linked with U.S. Special Forces. Both Director Tenet and Cofer Black, head of the Agency's Counterterrorism Center, emphasized that the war would be driven by intelligence, noting that locating the enemy would be the challenge.[125]

---

[120] U.S. Department of State, "Talking Point for PC: 0930 on 14 September 2001" (Washington DC, 2001), http://www.gwu.edu/~nsarchiv/NSAEBB/NSAEBB358a/doc07.pdf (accessed December 19, 2011)

[121] U.S. Department of State, "Action Plan as of 9/13/2001 7:55:51am" (Washington DC, Sept. 13, 2001), http://www.gwu.edu/~nsarchiv/NSAEBB/NSAEBB358a/doc01.pdf (accessed December 19, 2011).

[122] *The 9/11 Commission Report*, 327.

[123] Feith, *War and Decision*, 14.

[124] Tommy Franks, *American Soldier* (New York: ReganBooks, 2004), 250.

[125] Tenet, *At the Center of the Storm*, 176.

With the individual Department plans developing, the President took his National

Security team to Camp David on September 15, 2001 to develop the battle plan for

Afghanistan.[126] On 9/11, the President spoke with Secretary Rumsfeld from Barksdale Air Force

Base. In his memoirs, he recalled the conversation, "I told Don our first priority was to make it

through the immediate crisis. After that, I planned to mount a serious military response."[127] The

concept of that plan would be formed at Camp David. General Shelton presented United States

Central Command's options for the use of military force in Afghanistan. The three courses of

action included a limited cruise missile strike against al Qaeda training camps, more robust

bomber strikes in addition to cruise missile attacks, and a broader campaign combining ground

forces with air strikes.[128] In concert, the CIA then detailed their refined plan, in large part the

same plan the Agency had presented nearly a year earlier.[129] The key elements of their plan

included efforts to eliminate Afghanistan's safe haven, al Qaeda leadership, financial structure,

and to pursue al Qaeda in an additional 92 countries.[130]

After considering the opinions of his team, the President approved the CIA plan.[131] In

addition, on September 16, he decided on the military's 'boots on the ground' option.[132] While

deciding to send ground forces to Afghanistan, he was reluctant to commit to a subsequent

nation-building mission. From that guidance, following the defeat of al Qaeda and the Taliban,

the military planned to assume a support role to a presumed combination of other nations,

---

[126] Bush, *Decision Points*, 185.

[127] Ibid., 133.

[128] Richard B. Myers, *Eyes on the Horizon: Serving on the Front Lines of National Security* (New York: Threshold Editions, 2009), 166.

[129] Tenet, *At the Center of the Storm*, 131.

[130] Ibid., 178.

[131] Ibid., 131.

[132] Bush, *Decision Points*, 191.

international organizations and non-governmental organizations that would assume the lead.[133] To certify his intent, and largely consistent with the proposals discussed over the past week, the President issued written instructions to the Principals on September 17 to assign their 'War on Terrorism' tasks.[134]

Concluding the first week's planning efforts, Congress passed authorization legislation, and the President subsequently addressed the Congress with respect to his plan. On September 18, Congress passed a joint resolution granting the President the authority to act against those responsible for 9/11. Specifically, the resolution directed,

> The President is authorized to use all necessary and appropriate force against those nations, organizations, or persons he determines planned, authorized, committed, or aided the terrorist attacks that occurred on September 11, 2001, or harbored such organizations or persons, in order to prevent any future acts of international terrorism against the United States by such nations, organizations or persons.[135]

While granting broad authorities, the resolution did stipulate that actions had to be associated to the 9/11 attacks. On September 20, 2001, President Bush addressed Congress. He outlined a whole of government approach, stating, "We will direct every resource at our command – every means of diplomacy, every tool of intelligence, every instrument of law enforcement, every financial influence, and every necessary weapon of war – to the disruption and to the defeat of the global terror network."[136] While only granted authority to act against those responsible for 9/11, the President dictated his intent to achieve a much broader aim, defeating the 'global terror network.'

While the Cabinet departments conducted their initial planning, a parallel effort directed at Iraq, involving the Presidency and the Department of Defense, began to take shape. Following

---

[133] Myers, *Eyes on the Horizon*, 173-174.

[134] *The 9/11 Commission Report*, 333.

[135] *Authorization for Use of Military Force*, SJR 23, 107th Cong., 1st sess., *Congressional Record* 147, no. 120, daily ed. (September 14, 2001): S 9421.

[136] National Review, *"We Will Prevail"*, 14.

up on his query to Clarke the day prior, President Bush again raised the question of Iraq, and its possible connection to 9/11 and al Qaeda, during his September 13 National Security Council meeting.[137] Responding to the President, and emphasizing the difficulty of targeting al Qaeda in Afghanistan, Secretary Rumsfeld presented the option of Iraq due to their state sponsorship of terrorism, pursuit of weapons of mass destruction, and the notion of using action against Iraq as an example to other regimes. President Bush then declared that any action against Iraq would have to result in a change in government, and correspondingly directed Secretary Rumsfeld and General Shelton to develop a plan and cost estimate.[138]

In preparation for the September 15 Camp David meetings, Secretary Rumsfeld directed Under Secretary Feith and Peter Rodman, the Assistant Secretary of Defense for International Security Affairs, to draft a strategy memo to send to the attendees in advance. The memo proposed immediate targeting of al Qaeda, the Taliban, and Iraq. Iraq was named due to the threat of weapons of mass destruction terrorism and their systematic undermining of U.S. and United Nations efforts. The memo argued that action against Iraq could then serve as a deterrent against Libya and Syria.[139] Verbalizing this argument at the Camp David meeting, Deputy Secretary Wolfowitz conceptualized a war broader than Afghanistan alone, and in turn presented the case for Iraq.[140] In discussing his vision of an offensive strategy, with corresponding improvements in homeland security, Vice President Cheney voiced his concerns with regard to the weapons of mass destruction threat. While a proponent of action against Iraq, he argued for an 'Afghanistan first' strategy at Camp David. In his memoirs, he affirmed, "I believed it was important to deal

---

[137] Richard Clarke's matching account of this discussion placed it on September 12th versus September 13th.

[138] Feith, *War and Decision*, 14-15.

[139] Ibid., 50-52.

[140] Rumsfeld, *Known and Unknown*, 359.

31

with the threat Iraq posed."[141] The next day, September 16, President Bush decided against Iraq

as an initial target, choosing to focus first on Afghanistan.[142] However, on September 17,

confirming his verbal guidance to the Department of Defense on September 13, the President

signed a top secret terrorism document which included direction to the Pentagon to begin

development of military options for an invasion of Iraq.[143]

Simultaneous to the deliberations and resultant decisions of the policy-makers, the

Department of Defense and United States Central Command, following guidance from Vice

President Cheney, began to work on Iraq war plans nearly immediately in the weeks following

9/11.[144] To deliver the same directive, the President called Secretary Rumsfeld to a private

meeting in the Oval Office on September 26, where he asked Secretary Rumsfeld to review the

status of military plans for Iraq.[145] In turn, on September 29 and only eight days prior to the initial

air strikes in Afghanistan, Secretary Rumsfeld directed incoming Chairman of the Joint Chiefs of

Staff General Richard Myers to begin preparing military options for Iraq with the objectives of

finding and destroying weapons of mass destruction, and regime change.[146] At the same time, he

reminded General Tommy Franks, the commander of United States Central Command, during a

late September videoconference, "By the way, General, don't forget about Iraq." General Franks

acknowledged, "I won't, Mr. Secretary."[147] Displaying his acquiescence, General Franks stated in

---

[141] Richard B. Cheney, *In My Time: A Personal and Political Memoir* (New York: Threshold Editions, 2011), 333-334.

[142] Bush, *Decision Points*, 191.

[143] Glenn Kessler, "U.S. Decision On Iraq Has Puzzling Past: Opponents of War Wonder When, How Policy Was Set," *Washington Post*, January 12, 2003.

[144] Cheney, *In My Time*, 369.

[145] Rumsfeld, *Known and Unknown*, 425.

[146] Feith, *War and Decision*, 218.

[147] Franks, *American Soldier*, 268.

his memoirs, "Planning for that day (when America would change its containment strategy), I thought, was the only wise course of action."[148]

Two months later, on November 21, 2001, President Bush, again in private, asked Secretary Rumsfeld, "Where do we stand on the Iraq planning?"[149] To respond to the President's query, Secretary Rumsfeld called General Franks on November 27 and asked, "General Franks, the President wants us to look at options for Iraq. What is the status of your planning?"[150] He then gave General Franks a one-week suspense to reply. With the short suspense, United States Central Command began to plan for Iraq in earnest.[151] General Franks conducted his initial brief on the Iraq plan to Secretary Rumsfeld on December 4, 2001, then follow-up briefs on December 12 and December 19. Culminating these preparatory briefings, General Franks traveled to Crawford Ranch on December 28, 2001 to brief his initial Commander's Concept for military action against the Iraqi regime.[152]

While solely focusing his briefing on the operational aspects of the plan, General Franks missed his first opportunity to provide direct 'best military advice' to the President, and expand the discussion beyond operational concerns to the strategic concerns of 'why' and ramifications of an invasion of Iraq.[153] Further, the intense December planning effort for Iraq provided distraction to United States Central Command leadership as the Command planned for and executed the early-December Tora Bora battle, and unsuccessful attempt to kill or capture Osama bin Laden.[154] Continuing the focus on Iraq, and distraction from Afghanistan, General Franks and

---

[148] Franks, *American Soldier*, 268.

[149] Rumsfeld, *Known and Unknown*, 427.

[150] Franks, *American Soldier*, 315.

[151] Ibid.

[152] Ibid., 329-355.

[153] Myers, *Eyes on the Horizon*, 222.

[154] Dalton Fury, *Kill Bin Laden: A Delta Force Commander's Account of the Hunt for the World's Most Wanted Man* (New York: St. Martin's Griffin, 2008), 284-287.

his Operations Director, Major General Gene Renuart, traveled often to Washington DC over the course of the following two months to brief the status of Iraq planning.[155] Between December, 2001, and August, 2002, General Franks would brief the President more than a dozen times on the evolving Iraq battle plan.[156]

As evidenced, the administration's planning effort in the wake of 9/11 did result in a whole of government approach; however, the Cabinet departments' plans were not informed by an adequate explanation of the problem at hand, and were never fully integrated into a comprehensive and complementary strategy. Addressing this conclusion, Under Secretary Feith observed that, "The strategy would require many parts, public and private, U.S. and foreign. But no one took charge of this project for the U.S. government."[157] The administration also, with the exception of the Department of State, generally disregarded consideration of bin Laden's motivations, or terrorism causes as a whole. Recalling the administration's initial deliberations, Under Secretary Feith did note the State Department's persistent argument for addressing the root causes of terrorism; however, he at the same time discredited this argument, saying it "tended to produce paralysis rather than motivate action against terrorist extremist ideology."[158] Finally, marginalizing Director Tenet's insistence that, "Let me say it again: CIA found absolutely no linkage between Saddam and 9/11," the administration promoted a divergent and distracting strategy, pursuing planning efforts against the Iraqi regime.[159]

---

[155] Myers, *Eyes on the Horizon*, 224.

[156] Bush, *Decision Points*, 235.

[157] Feith, *War and Decision*, 170.

[158] Ibid., 170.

[159] Tenet, *At the Center of the Storm*, 341.

Influences on Presidential Decision-Making

In addition to the lack of focus and understanding of the threat, the basic fundamentals of the administration's decision-making apparatus profoundly influenced the resultant strategy. President Bush entered the Oval Office with no federal government experience, and a limited background in national defense and foreign policy.[160] To offset these limitations, sound Cabinet staff and National Security Council guidance would be required to advise and assist the President's policymaking. This necessary guidance was hindered by the President's decisive and aggressive decision-making style which was limited in its dependence on outside counsel. Further, counsel that the President did seek was from a narrow set of advisors. Finally, the National Security Council was constrained by their procedures, and hindered by critical personnel turnover.

President Bush was a decisive decision-maker, relying on instinct and intuition rather than analysis and deliberation. Author Bob Woodward, through personal observation reflected that, "Bush's leadership style bordered on the hurried. He wanted action, solutions."[161] Secretary Rumsfeld reached a similar conclusion, stating, "In my view the President did not always receive, and may not have insisted on, a timely consideration of his options before he made a decision."[162] Secretary O'Neill described a sort of detached style where the President would avoid conversation, questioning, or debate on policy matters. Unlike his sessions with former Presidents Nixon, Ford, Bush Sr., and Clinton, which were characterized by robust engagement, his meetings with President Bush followed a monologue format versus a dialogue.[163] Summarizing the President's preference for action versus analysis, Clarke concluded that, "The problem was

---

[160] Michael Beschloss and Hugh Sidey, "The White House," http://www.whitehouse.gov/about/presidents/georgewbush (accessed January 12, 2012).

[161] Bob Woodward, *Bush at War* (New York: Simon & Schuster, 2002), 256.

[162] Rumsfeld, *Known and Unknown*, 318.

[163] Ron Suskind, *The Price of Loyalty: George Bush, the White House, and the Education of Paul O'Neill* (New York: Simon & Schuster, 2004), 58.

that many of the important issues, like terrorism, like Iraq, were laced with important subtlety and nuance. These issues needed analysis and Bush and his inner circle had no real interest in complicated analyses; on the issues that they cared about, they already knew the answers, it was received wisdom."[164]

In addition to an aggressive decision-making style, President Bush did not seek a wide array of counsel. Clarke observed that, "Bush was informed by talking with a small set of senior advisors."[165] Through his research, Dale Herspring reached a similar conclusion. In analyzing President Bush's leadership style, he found that, "The heads of these (Cabinet) departments were autonomous, and the president dealt almost exclusively with them."[166]

Exacerbating the dependence on a narrow set of advisors, Secretary O'Neill observed a climate where the highly experienced defense team was able to exert undue influence over the new, and inexperienced, President. Documenting Secretary O'Neill's experience, author Ron Suskind dictated, "It was a broken process, O'Neill thought, or rather no process at all; there seemed to be no apparatus to assess policy and deliberate effectively, to create coherent governance."[167] As a result, Secretary O'Neill further held that, "Bush's leadership style allowed Rumsfeld to dominate the formulation of national security policy."[168] Demonstrating this weighted advisory dependence, the *Washington Post* found a linkage to the administration's decision-making with respect to Iraq. Through a series of interviews concerning the post-9/11 decision to pursue regime change in Iraq, they found that "the decision to confront Hussein at this time emerged in an ad hoc fashion. Often, the process circumvented traditional policymaking

---

[164] Clarke, *Against All Enemies*, 243.

[165] Ibid., 243.

[166] Dale R. Herspring, *The Pentagon and the Presidency: Civil-Military Relations from FDR to George W. Bush* (Lawrence, Kansas: University Press of Kansas, 2005), 378.

[167] Suskind, *The Price of Loyalty*, 97.

[168] Herspring, *The Pentagon and the Presidency*, 379.

channels as longtime advocates of ousting Hussein pushed Iraq to the top of the agenda by connecting their cause to the war on terrorism."[169]

Compounding the decision-making restrictions imposed by the President's leadership style, the National Security Council process was limited in its effectiveness. The early precedent of National Security Council meetings was one of strict format and limited debate. Secretary O'Neill recalled his amazement that the National Security Council sessions were scripted with little engagement from the President. Each attendee was told beforehand what to talk about, when, and for how long.[170]

Trained to this format which left no room for deliberation and debate, the staff appeared to be unprepared for the challenge of post-9/11 policymaking. At the critical Camp David meetings, where the initial post-9/11 policy would be debated, General Myers described the talks as "loose brainstorming sessions," versus "structured policy presentations."[171] Similarly, Secretary Rumsfeld critiqued the lack of an overarching strategy with regards to Afghanistan. He highlighted the fact that Iran and Russia had Afghanistan strategies but the United States did not. He blamed the interagency process, and specifically the slowness of the Deputies Committee to produce results.[172] Finally, Under Secretary Feith criticized both process and resourcing. He described a National Security Council that saw the necessity of efforts from all elements of national power; however, he stated, "The war exposed the maddening difficulty of getting the different parts of the U.S. government to work together in joint operations. In general, they lacked

---

[169] Kessler, "U.S. Decision On Iraq Has Puzzling Past".

[170] Suskind, *The Price of Loyalty*, 147-148.

[171] Myers, *Eyes on the Horizon*, 165.

[172] Donald Rumsfeld, "Afghanistan," Snowflake to Doug Feith (Washington DC, April 17, 2002), http://www.gwu.edu/~nsarchiv/NSAEBB/NSAEBB358a/doc23.pdf (accessed December 19, 2011).

experience in such operations and lacked the proper organization, personnel, and contracting

policies to carry them out. They did not train for such operations, and had no budget to do so."[173]

Typical of Presidential administration changes, the National Security Council's personnel

experienced significant turnover in 2001, with two significant changes in the immediate aftermath

of 9/11. Richard Clarke held the primary counterterrorism position in the Clinton administration,

and was maintained in that position by the new administration, providing crucial continuity.

However, in early October, 2001, after nine years in the position, his responsibilities were shifted

to Cyberspace Security. His replacement, retired General Wayne Downing, former commander of

U.S. Special Operations Command, then resigned in June, 2002 due to alleged frustration with the

administration's bureaucratic response to the threat. Next, Randy Beers and John Gordon jointly

assumed the position, with Beers resigning in March, 2003, citing the administration's

prioritization of the Iraq War over vigorous pursuit of al Qaeda. Gordon departed in June, 2003 to

become the Homeland Security Advisor.[174]

The second significant change was the Chairman of the Joint Chiefs of Staff position

which was in transition at the time of the attacks. In September, 2001, General Shelton was

handing the position over to General Myers, leaving a potential continuity gap for the President's

principal military advisor.[175] Symptomatic of the transition, Secretary Rumsfeld stated, "The

shock of 9/11 had not provoked much originality or imagination from the Chairman or his

staff."[176] Further, he critiqued the lack of creativity of the military to produce a range of options.

In an October 10, 2001 memo to General Myers, he criticized, "DoD has produced next to no

actionable suggestions as to how we can assist in applying the urgently needed pressure on

---

[173] Feith, *War and Decision*, 86-87.

[174] Clarke, *Against All Enemies*, 240-242.

[175] General Myers was notified of his selection to be the Chairman on August 23, 2001, and was sworn in on October 1, 2001.

[176] Rumsfeld, *Known and Unknown*, 358-359.

terrorists other than cruise missiles and bombs."[177] President Bush's predisposition toward action over analysis, coupled with self-imposed and organizational counsel limitations, facilitated the evolution of a broad versus focused response to 9/11.

Resultant Strategy

The grand strategy that would define the War on Terror was largely established with President Bush's rapid decisions on 9/11 that we had entered a war, it would be against terrorism, and it would include state sponsors in its target set. In his memoirs, President Bush detailed the strategy he developed, naming it "the Bush Doctrine: First, make no distinction between the terrorists and the nations that harbor them – and hold both to account. Second, take the fight to the enemy overseas before they can attack us again here at home. Third, confront threats before they fully materialize. And fourth, advance liberty and hope as an alternative to the enemy's ideology of repression and fear."[178] In addition to the pursuit of state sponsors, the doctrine incorporated an offensive, preemptive approach, and the idealist element of spreading American values.

President Bush's idealist tendency played an important role in determining the strategy. Merriam-Webster defines a realist as one who has "concern for fact or reality and rejection of the impractical and visionary."[179] On the contrary, an idealist is "one that places ideals before practical considerations."[180] President Bush displayed his idealist mindset in pursuing the goal of ending global terrorism, versus taking a realist approach, and focusing the nation's efforts on the more achievable goal of confronting bin Laden and al Qaeda.

---

[177] Donald Rumsfeld, "What Will be the Military Role in the War on Terrorism," Snowflake to General Myers (Washington DC, October 10, 2001), http://www rumsfeld.com/endnotes/chapter-28/ (accessed December 20, 2011).

[178] Bush, *Decision Points*, 396-397.

[179] *Merriam-Webster Online*, s.v. "realist," http://www merriam-webster.com/dictionary/realist (accessed January 13, 2012).

[180] *Merriam-Webster Online*, s.v. "idealist," http://www.merriam-webster.com/dictionary/idealist (accessed January 13, 2012).

Speaking to the press corps on September 13, 2001, the President stated, "Now is an opportunity to do generations a favor, by coming together and whipping terrorism; hunting it down, finding it and holding them accountable."[181] Defending the invasion of Iraq, his memoirs discussed the impact on combating extremists, "The best way to protect our countries in the long run was to counter their dark vision with a more compelling alternative. That alternative was freedom."[182] Finally, discussing the fourth pillar of the 'Bush Doctrine,' he contended, "The Freedom Agenda, as I called the fourth prong, was both idealistic and realistic." He continued, "It was realistic because freedom is the most practical way to protect our country in the long run. As I said in my Second Inaugural Address, 'America's vital interests and our deepest beliefs are now one.'"[183] Undoubtedly, the President's idealist worldview exerted significant influence over all aspects of the 'Bush Doctrine.'

This section will begin by detailing the strategy that evolved from 9/11 to the President's Address to Congress on September 20, 2001. It will then examine the evolution of the strategy through a series of defining speeches in 2001 and 2002 that led to the publishing of the September 2002 National Security Strategy. Finally, the section will document the significant actions that were taken in execution of the strategy.

Early Formulation of Strategy

Before examining the evolution of the post-9/11 grand strategy, it is instructive to look back at the early policy discussions that occurred under the Bush administration prior to 9/11. President Bush held his first National Security Council meeting on January 30, 2001. During this meeting, Secretary O'Neill immediately sensed a shift in America's Middle East policy, a combination of disengagement from the Israeli-Palestinian conflict, and refocus on Iraq.

---

[181] Fleischer, *Taking Heat*, 160.

[182] Bush, *Decision Points*, 232.

[183] Ibid., 397.

Referring to the Israeli-Palestinian conflict, and the breakdown of peace talks at the end of the Clinton administration, Bush stated, "I don't see much we can do over there at this point. I think it's time to pull out of that situation."[184] The meeting then turned to Iraq. The President directed Secretary Powell to craft new sanctions, Secretary Rumsfeld to examine military options, and Director Tenet to improve intelligence with respect to Iraq.[185]

Two days later, President Bush held his second National Security Council meeting. Again, the topic of the meeting was Iraq, with regime change as an agenda item.[186] From the outset, the focus of the administration appeared to be Iraq. Echoing this sentiment, Secretary O'Neill recalled that, "From the start, we were building the case against Hussein and looking at how we could take him out and change Iraq into a new country."[187] Under Secretary Feith likewise witnessed the emphasis toward Iraq. Discussing the post-9/11 deliberations, which included Iraq, he stated, "Administration officials had been discussing Iraq policy options for months."[188] Given the pre-9/11 administration focus on Iraq, inclusion as a component of the post-9/11 strategy was, in a sense, preordained.

The framework of the 'Bush Doctrine' was set with immediacy after the 9/11 attacks. On that day, President Bush decided to target terrorism, versus bin Laden and al Qaeda, and pursue state sponsors. Reflecting on his thoughts on 9/11, he recalled, "I did want to announce a major decision I had made: the United States would consider any nation that harbored terrorists to be responsible for the acts of those terrorists."[189] He made this proclamation to the nation in his Presidential Address that evening, stating, "We will make no distinction between the terrorists

---

[184] Suskind, *The Price of Loyalty*, 71.

[185] Ibid., 72-75.

[186] Ibid., 82-85.

[187] Ibid., 86.

[188] Feith, *War and Decision*, 14.

[189] Bush, *Decision Points*, 137.

who committed these acts and those who harbor them."[190] He then reaffirmed his intent to broaden the scope of his response beyond bin Laden and al Qaeda, stating, "We stand together to win the war against terrorism."[191] From day one of the conflict, the President's intended response reflected a decoupling of the strategy we would pursue from the actual threat presented to us. Exemplifying this observation, Secretary Rumsfeld, in his memoirs, stated his viewpoint, "Nor was this struggle simply about apprehending one man – Osama bin Laden – or one organization – al-Qaida. The task we faced was about systematically pressuring, attacking, and disrupting terrorist networks worldwide."[192]

Culminating the first week after 9/11, and presenting the basis of his strategy, President Bush addressed Congress on September 20, 2001. Making clear his intent to expand the strategic aims beyond bin Laden and al Qaeda, he announced, "Our war on terror begins with al Qaeda, but it does not end there. It will not end until every terrorist group of global reach has been found, stopped, and defeated."[193] He then stated his commitment to hold state sponsors to account, stating, "From this day forward, any nation that continues to harbor or support terrorism will be regarded by the United States as a hostile regime."[194] These pillars of the 'Bush Doctrine' would remain consistent as the strategy later evolved to include an offensive and preemptive element, as well as an incorporation of the 'Freedom Agenda.'

Refinement and Documentation

The month of September, 2001 concluded with noteworthy steps across the U.S. government being taken against al Qaeda and the Taliban in Afghanistan, most significantly the

---

[190] National Review, *"We Will Prevail"*, 3.

[191] Ibid., 3.

[192] Rumsfeld, *Known and Unknown*, 356.

[193] National Review, *"We Will Prevail"*, 14.

[194] Ibid., 15.

preparation for the pending military campaign. These attacks began on the night of October 7, 2001. That afternoon, Secretary Rumsfeld and General Myers held a press briefing to detail the military objectives of the Afghanistan campaign. After listing his desired military outcomes, Secretary Rumsfeld confirmed that the overall effort to combat terrorism would not be confined to Afghanistan, stating, "While our raids today focus on the Taliban and the foreign terrorists in Afghanistan, our aim remains much broader. Our objective is to defeat those who use terrorism and those who house or support them." He continued, "We share the belief that terrorism is a cancer on the human condition and we intend to oppose it wherever it is."[195]

Two months later, after marked progress in Afghanistan, the President addressed the Citadel Cadets in Charleston, South Carolina on December 11, 2001. In this speech, he continued his consistent message to oppose state sponsorship of terrorism, stating, "Above all, we're acting to end the state sponsorship of terror. Rogue states are clearly the most likely sources of chemical and biological and nuclear weapons for terrorists."[196] Referring to these terrorist sponsoring states, he then proclaimed, "They have been warned, they are being watched, and they will be held to account."[197] This statement, three weeks after requesting an update on Iraq planning from Secretary Rumsfeld, and with the United States Central Command Commander's Concept for Iraq in development, alluded to the inclusion of preemption in the 'Bush Doctrine'.

In his 2002 State of the Union Address, President Bush became explicit in his intention to preempt apparent state sponsors. In preparing for the 2002 State of the Union Address, David Frum recalled his assignment from Michael Gerson, President Bush's chief speechwriter, "Can you sum up in a sentence or two our best case for going after Iraq?"[198] From Frum's perspective,

---

[195] Donald Rumsfeld, "Rumsfeld and Myers Briefing on Enduring Freedom" (press statement, Pentagon, Washington DC, October 7, 2001).

[196] National Review, *"We Will Prevail"*, 91.

[197] Ibid.

[198] Frum, *The Right Man*, 224.

"His request to me could not have been simpler: I was to provide a justification for a war."[199] President Bush detailed this justification in his Address, stating his intent to pursue "two great objectives. First, we will shut down terrorist camps, disrupt terrorist plans, and bring terrorists to justice. And, second, we must prevent the terrorists and regimes who seek chemical, biological, or nuclear weapons from threatening the United States and the world."[200] He then introduced his 'axis of evil' trinity of North Korea, Iran, and Iraq, and described their pursuit of weapons of mass destruction. Directed at these nations, he stated, "I will not wait on events, while dangers gather. I will not stand by, as peril draws closer and closer."[201]

Four months later, President Bush confirmed his strategy of offense and preemption, addressing the West Point graduating class on June 1, 2002. Again, describing the threatening combination of rogue regimes and weapons of mass destruction, he stated, "Containment is not possible when unbalanced dictators with weapons of mass destruction can deliver those weapons on missiles or secretly provide them to terrorist allies."[202] Declaring his intent to be preemptive, he continued, "If we wait for threats to fully materialize, we will have waited too long."[203] Finally, proclaiming the necessity of taking the offensive, he stated, "In the world we have entered, the only path to safety is the path of action. And this nation will act."[204] Three months later, President Bush documented his grand strategy in the 2002 National Security Strategy.

A year after the 9/11 attacks, the nation's grand strategy, known as the 'Bush Doctrine,' was published with the release of the 2002 National Security Strategy. Incorporating the 'Freedom Agenda,' the strategy is founded on an emphasis toward pursuing democracy, liberty

---

[199] Frum, *The Right Man*, 224.

[200] National Review, *"We Will Prevail"*, 107.

[201] Ibid., 108.

[202] National Review, *"We Will Prevail"*, 160.

[203] Ibid.

[204] Ibid.

and hope, stating, "In pursuit of our goals, our first imperative is to clarify what we stand for: the United States must defend liberty and justice because these principles are right and true for all people everywhere."[205] Next, the strategy reaffirmed the President's intent to hold both terrorists and their state sponsors to account, stating, "We make no distinction between terrorists and those who knowingly harbor or provide aid to them."[206] The strategy then made the argument for preemption. First, the introduction identified that the "gravest danger our Nation faces lies at the crossroads of radicalism and technology," with technology referring to weapons of mass destruction.[207] Then referring to these weapons, and demonstrating the doctrine of preemption, the strategy continued, "As a matter of common sense and self-defense, America will act against such emerging threats before they are fully formed."[208] Finally, culminating the argument, the strategy declared, "To forestall or prevent such hostile acts by our adversaries, the United States will, if necessary, act preemptively."[209]

Whole of Government Execution

While strategy development in the aftermath of 9/11 largely focused on broad military solutions to combat terrorism, the resultant execution did include efforts across the whole of government. These actions included improved homeland security and homeland defense, diplomacy, intelligence reform, aggressive law enforcement, and terrorist financing measures.

Immediately following the 9/11 attacks, necessary action was taken to improve the nation's homeland security and homeland defense. The first, and most obvious, measure was to improve air security. On September 19, 2001, a government job announcement was posted

---

[205] U.S. President, *The National Security Strategy of the United States of America* (Washington DC, 2002), 3.

[206] Ibid., 5.

[207] Ibid., ii.

[208] Ibid., ii.

[209] Ibid., 15.

45

seeking Federal Air Marshal candidates.[210] Within ten months, the number of Federal Air Marshals in service grew from fewer than fifty to thousands.[211] Correspondingly, the Federal Air Marshal Service annual budget grew from 4.4 million dollars for fiscal year 2001 to 545 million dollars for fiscal year 2003.[212] Later, on November 19, 2001, the *Aviation and Transportation Security Act of 2001* created the Transportation Security Administration. While responsible for securing all modes of transportation, the agency's primary mission would be aviation security.[213]

Homeland security and homeland defense continued to be a priority in 2002. The 2002 Unified Command Plan designated a new area of responsibility and respective combatant command, United States Northern Command, to plan, organize, and execute homeland defense missions. The command was established on October 1, 2002.[214] The next month, Congress acted to secure the maritime environment. To provide greater security for the nation's seaports and waterways, the President signed the *Maritime Transportation Security Act of 2002* on November 25, 2002.[215] The same day, the President culminated his homeland security agenda by signing the *Homeland Security Act of 2002*. The act created the Department of Homeland Security, with a respective Secretary of Homeland Security, to "prevent terrorist attacks within the United States," and to "reduce the vulnerability of the United States to terrorism."[216]

---

[210] U.S. General Accounting Office, *Aviation Security: Federal Air Marshal Service is Addressing Challenges of its Expanded Mission and Workforce, but Additional Actions Needed* (Washington DC, November 2003) 38.

[211] Ibid., 1.

[212] Ibid., 6.

[213] *Aviation and Transportation Security Act of 2001*, Public Law 107-71, 107th Cong., 1st sess. (November 19, 2001).

[214] U.S. Northern Command, "About USNORTHCOM," http://www northcom.mil/About/index.html (accessed 29 January, 2012).

[215] *Maritime Transportation Security Act of 2002*, Public Law 107-295, 107th Cong., 2nd sess. (November 25, 2002).

[216] *Homeland Security Act of 2002*, Public Law 107-296, § 101-102, 107th Cong., 2d sess. (November 25, 2002).

Critical to prosecuting a global war against terrorism, the administration sought to build a global coalition of nations. In the first eight months following 9/11, President Bush met with the leaders of over fifty nations to forge this global coalition against terrorism. At the same time, senior members of the Departments of State and Defense, as well as the CIA traveled to every continent to pursue the same goal.[217] Displaying the unity of nations in the aftermath of 9/11, the United Nations Security Council passed Resolution 1373 on September 28, 2001. This far-reaching edict directed all member nations to take actions to prevent terrorist financing. It further called on all nations to improve information sharing, border security, and law enforcement cooperation with respect to terrorism.[218] Demonstrating further unity, over ninety nations endorsed the Proliferation Security Initiative, introduced by President Bush on May 31, 2003. The Initiative sought to interdict transfers of weapons of mass destruction materials, and to develop information-sharing procedures to facilitate interdiction.[219]

To address intelligence limitations, considered by many to be the primary shortfall identified by 9/11, several actions were taken to improve collection and, most importantly, sharing. First, the *United and Strengthening America by Providing Appropriate Tools Required to Intercept and Obstruct Terrorism Act of 2001*, known as the Patriot Act, was signed into law on October 26, 2001. This wide-ranging act enabled information-sharing between law enforcement and intelligence agencies, facilitated monitoring of terrorist communications, assisted law enforcement in investigating and prosecuting suspected terrorists, and granted authorities to combat terrorist financing.[220] To further exploit terrorist communications, the National Security

---

[217] U.S. Department of State, *Patterns of Global Terrorism* (Washington, DC, 2001), vi.

[218] United Nations Security Council, 4,385th meeting, Official Records, *Security Council Resolution 1373 (2001)* (New York, September 28, 2001).

[219] "Proliferation Security Initiative," May 31, 2003, http://www.state.gov/t/isn/c10390.htm (accessed 23 December, 2011).

[220] *United and Strengthening America by Providing Appropriate Tools Required to Intercept and Obstruct Terrorism (USA PATRIOT) Act of 2001*, Public Law 107-56, 107th Cong., 1st sess. (October 26, 2001).

Agency implemented its Terrorist Surveillance Program to monitor international communications associated with al Qaeda.[221] Next, the intelligence community's Terrorist Threat Integration Center opened on May 1, 2003. This center brought analysts from the Departments of State, Defense, Justice, and Homeland Security, as well as the Intelligence Community together for the specific purpose of sharing and fusing terrorist intelligence.[222] The center was later renamed the National Counterterrorism Center.[223] Finally, President Bush established a Director of National Intelligence to coordinate the entirety of the intelligence community.[224]

The Departments of Justice and Treasury took equally important measures to interdict and preempt future terrorist attacks. The FBI undertook a sweeping transformation from their previous investigatory framework to a preventative mindset. The FBI's counterterrorism efforts prior to 9/11 were focused on investigating and prosecuting terrorist incidents after the fact. After 9/11, the Bureau's "top priority became the prevention of another terrorist attack."[225] To address terrorist financing, the President issued Executive Order 13224 on September 24, 2001. This order blocked all named terrorist property, interests, and transactions in the United States, and called for the Secretary of State and Secretary of Treasury to coordinate and cooperate with other nations to deny terrorist financing.[226]

---

[221] Tenet, *At the Center of the Storm*, 237.

[222] Central Intelligence Agency, "Terrorist Threat Integration Center Begins Operations," https://www.cia.gov/news-information/press-releases-statements/press-release-archive-2003/pr05012003.html (accessed January 29, 2012).

[223] Executive Order no. 13354, *Code of Federal Regulations*, title 3, p. 214 (2005).

[224] *Intelligence Reform and Terrorism Prevention Act of 2004*, Public Law 108-458, 108th Cong., 2nd sess. (December 17, 2004).

[225] Robert S. Mueller, III , "The FBI Transformation Since 2001" (remarks before the House Appropriations Subcommittee on Science, the Departments of State, Justice and Commerce, and Related Agencies, Washington DC, September 14, 2001).

[226] Executive Order no. 13224, *Code of Federal Regulations*, title 3, p. 786 (2002).

The military component of the strategy focused on the Afghanistan, and later Iraq, campaigns. Based on the Congressional *Authorization for Use of Military Force*,[227] the United States, along with a fifty-five nation coalition initiated Operation Enduring Freedom on October 7, 2001 against al Qaeda and the Taliban in Afghanistan.[228] One year later, on October 16, 2002, Congress authorized military force against Iraq, which was initiated with Operation Iraqi Freedom on March 20, 2003.[229] In addition to the Afghanistan and Iraq campaigns, the United States executed lesser known military training missions in Yemen, the Philippines, and Georgia, training their respective counterterrorism forces to fight al Qaeda on their soil.[230] While the nation's strategy weighted heavily toward the military component, significant contributions were made by all the elements of national power.

Consequences of Executed Strategy

The previous chapter detailed the broad and unfocused strategy that was adopted in response to 9/11. By its design, and breadth, the resultant strategy did not specifically concentration on bin Laden and al Qaeda threat, or consider their motives in prosecuting the 9/11 attacks. Cautioning against "disproportionately counterproductive and irrational responses" to terrorism, Sherle Schwenninger contended, "It is nearly impossible not to give into the temptation, but it is strategically wise not to do so. By virtually any rational standard, terrorism does not warrant a full-scale war, let alone to be the defining feature of American grand strategy."[231] In the aftermath of 9/11, it was this very 'full-scale war' that the administration

---

[227] *Authorization for Use of Military Force*, SJR 23, 107th Cong., 1st sess., *Congressional Record* 147, no. 120, daily ed. (September 14, 2001): S 9421.

[228] U.S. Department of State, *Patterns of Global Terrorism* (Washington, DC, 2001), xiii.

[229] *Authorization for Use of Military Force Against Iraq Resolution of 2002*, Public Law 107-243, 107th Cong., 2nd sess. (October 16, 2002).

[230] U.S. Department of State, *Patterns of Global Terrorism* (Washington, DC, 2001), xiii.

[231] Sherle R. Schwenninger, "Revamping American Grand Strategy," *World Policy Journal* 20, no.3 (Fall 2003): 26.

chose to pursue. Concurrently, the administration failed to appreciate the enemy's perspective in designing the strategy. In his study of the cause-effect relationship of socio-economic, literacy, democratic, and extremism factors on Middle Eastern terrorism, Abdullah Mohammad found none to be compelling. Instead, he attributed American foreign policy in the Middle East. He summarized, "It is this very targeting of the *Ummah*, the historically united Islamic entity, which has delivered the people of the region into the arms of the Islamists. If the West fails to understand this elemental truth, we can only look forward to a future of greater terrorism."[232]

This section will first examine alternative strategies that were advocated for, and available to the administration. While innumerable revisionist strategies have been published and presented in the years since 9/11, this section will concentrate on those offered before or during the strategy-making process. The section will then review both the positive and negative results of the strategy that was ultimately executed.

Alternative Suggested Strategies

The preponderance of alternative approaches to combating terrorism in the aftermath of 9/11 were grounded on soft power capabilities. Contrary to these approaches, the United States executed a strategy centered on hard power, with robust military campaigns in Afghanistan and Iraq. These strategic choices exemplified the 'Bush Doctrine' tenets of offensive, preemptive action against purported state sponsors of terrorism. Regarding the invasion of Iraq, Daniel Byman cautioned, "Most important, the United States must strive to avoid the self-fulfilling prophecy that bin Laden and other insurgents want to create: to provoke a heavy-handed U.S. response to terrorism and then exploit it to generate more support for the overall cause."[233] A

---

[232] Abdullah Yousef Sahar Mohammad, "Roots of Terrorism in the Middle East: Internal Pressures and International Constraints," in *Root Causes of Terrorism: Myths, Reality, and Ways Forward*, ed. Tore Bjørgo (New York: Routledge, 2006), 108.

[233] Daniel L. Byman, "Al-Qaeda as an Adversary: Do We Understand Our Enemy?" *World Politics* 56 (October 2003): 161.

survey of suggested strategies reveals a near unanimous emphasis on soft power, leveraging governmental and public diplomacy, law enforcement, intelligence, foreign policy, coalition-building, and homeland defense. At the same time, these strategies advocated for limited use of military power focused on the al Qaeda threat. While there was a minority opinion that advocated for strong military involvement, such as Kenneth Pollack's *The Threatening Storm: The Case for Invading Iraq*, soft power was the majority opinion from a wide range of prominent think tanks and academics.[234]

Numerous governmental and think tank reports, available before and immediately after 9/11, emphasized soft power approaches versus reliance on military power. In their report *Terrorism, the Future, and U.S. Foreign Policy*, updated two days after 9/11, the Congressional Research Service outlined proposed policy options spanning from diplomacy, engagement, and sanctions, to law enforcement and military action. However, when discussing military action, the report cited numerous caveats and warnings, such as presupposition of the terrorist organization's location, potential for military and foreign civilian casualties, holding the wrong party responsible, and creating a perception that the United States ignores international law.[235]

Similar recommendations were presented by Sandia National Laboratories in their 1999 case study of bin Laden, and the RAND Corporation. Sandia's roadmap for countering the al Qaeda threat concentrated on the soft power elements of diplomacy, intelligence, law enforcement, strategic communications, image building, and legal efforts. Their study did offer military options, including the direct targeting of bin Laden, but was explicit in labeling international diplomacy as "the single most effective tool at our disposal."[236] Later, in RAND

---

[234] Kenneth M. Pollock, *The Threatening Storm: The Case for Invading Iraq* (New York: Random House, 2002), xiv.

[235] Congressional Research Service, *Terrorism, the Future, and U.S. Foreign Policy*, Raphael F. Perl (Washington DC, Sept. 13, 2001).

[236] Sandia National Laboratories, *Osama bin Laden: A Case Study*, 52-57.

testimony before the 9/11 Commission, Brian Jenkins suggested that the goals of our counterterrorism strategy should be to "keep the focus on terrorism," versus expanding to rogue governments, and to "keep the focus on destroying Al Qaeda."[237] He further testified to the need for fostering international cooperation, facilitating resolution of conflicts that provide breeding grounds for terrorism, and improving intelligence.[238]

On September 19, 2001, the bipartisan foreign policy think tank, Center for Strategic and International Studies, published one of the most direct rebukes against the use of hard power and military force in response to 9/11. While acknowledging the necessity to target the al Qaeda network, as well as their finances and state sponsorship, the proposed strategy called for diplomacy, intelligence, counter-proliferation, and homeland defense.[239] Regarding potential military action, the report cautioned, "We also cannot afford to engage in sweeping adventures such as military efforts to achieve regime change, unless this is clearly justified by direct responsibility for the attack."[240] Further, the report was explicit in encouraging focus in strategy deliberations, stating, "Persistence must be supported by a careful focus on those whom we can show to be truly guilty, and we must act in ways that carefully consider the post-attack political impact of each action."[241] The argument continued, "Our primary objective must be those terrorist directly involved in the attacks, and any cells and organizations associate with them."[242] Finally, addressing the potential intent to broaden the response beyond the immediate threat, the report opined, "Invasions and efforts at regime change are a last resort. We must avoid military

---

[237] Brian M. Jenkins, "Remarks before the National Commission on Terrorist Attacks Upon the United States" (testimony presented to the National Commission on Terrorist Attacks Upon the United States, Washington DC, March 31, 2003).

[238] Ibid.

[239] Anthony H. Cordesman and Arleigh A. Burke, *A New US Strategy for Counter-Terrorism and Asymmetric Warfare* (Washington DC: Center for Strategic and International Studies, 2001), 2.

[240] Ibid., 3.

[241] Ibid., 3.

[242] Ibid., 4.

adventures and reacting to special interests. These include 'lobbies' calling for regime change in Afghanistan and Iraq."[243]

Consistent with the predominant viewpoint of the think tank community, the array of academic counsel focused on soft power as well. Underpinning this theme, a 1993 reflection on twenty-five years of counterterrorism responses by Ronald Crelinsten and Alex Schmid argued strongly against military approaches to counterterrorism, citing that military responses had limited effectiveness in the historical record. They contended that hard line responses could play into the long-term strategy of the terrorists, and could facilitate terrorist recruitment and support. Further, they maintained that a perception of symmetry, derived from a military response, could serve to legitimize the terrorists, and that military responses often produced unintended consequences.[244]

Terrorism experts Bruce Hoffman, Thomas Mockaitis, and Daniel Byman consistently lobbied for approaches based on improved intelligence and public diplomacy. Hoffman, testifying before Congress in March, 2001, highlighted the "conspicuous absence of an overarching strategy" to combat terrorism. To frame future strategy, he called for a "comprehensive net assessment of the terrorist threat," the latest of which had not occurred in over six years.[245] After 9/11, he continued to promote intelligence improvements and reform as the basis for our strategy, testifying before Congress multiple times in the immediate weeks following the attacks.[246]

---

[243] Cordesman, *A New US Strategy for Counter-Terrorism and Asymmetric Warfare*, 4.

[244] Ronald D. Crelinsten and Alex P. Schmid, eds., *Western Responses to Terrorism* (London, England: Frank Cass, 1993), 317-319.

[245] Bruce Hoffman, "Combating Terrorism: In Search of a National Strategy" (testimony presented before the House Committee on Government Reform, Subcommittee on National Security, Veterans Affairs, and International Relations, Washington DC, March 27, 2001).

[246] Bruce Hoffman, "Preparing for the War on Terrorism" (testimony presented before the House Committee on Government Reform, Subcommittee on National Security, Veterans Affairs, and International Relations, Washington DC, September, 2001), and "Re-thinking Terrorism in Light of a War on Terrorism" (testimony presented before the House Permanent Select Committee on Intelligence, Subcommittee on Terrorism and Homeland Security, Washington DC, September 26, 2001).

Mockaitis also contended that improved intelligence was the critical component toward defeating al Qaeda. Further, he argued for public diplomacy efforts, which could lead to increased intelligence opportunities, and making reasonable adjustments to U.S. foreign policy in the Middle East to address grievances and serve as a mechanism to foster increased cooperation, and thus intelligence.[247] Similarly, Byman concentrated on public diplomacy as an essential strategy component, calling on the United States to be tireless in highlighting the poor results of Islamic governments in Afghanistan and Sudan to counter al Qaeda's promises and claims.[248]

While offering further soft power strategies, Barry Posen, Madeleine Albright, and Rohan Gunaratna warned against a broad campaign, instead proffering narrow, focused efforts against bin Laden and al Qaeda. Posen called for a strategy specifically focused on al Qaeda and its support network. Components of his strategy included diplomacy, coalition-building, intelligence, and special operations-focused military action.[249] Regarding broadening of the strategy beyond al Qaeda and Afghanistan, and referring to recommendations for action against Iraq, he questioned, "Perhaps the strangest advice is rumored to have come from Paul Wolfowitz, the U.S. deputy secretary of defense. He seems to believe that the time is ripe to deal with all of the United States' enemies and problems in the Middle East and Persian Gulf." He then continued, "But going after all of them now looks too much like a script written by al-Qaeda propagandists."[250]

Albright reinforced the imperative of focus in her testimony before the 9/11 Commission:

We were not attacked on September 11th by a noun, terrorism. We were attacked by individuals affiliated with al Qaeda. They are the enemies who killed our fellow citizens and foreigners, and defeating them should be the focus of our policy. If we pursue goals that are unnecessarily broad, such as the elimination not only of threats but also of

---

[247] Thomas R. Mockaitis and Paul B. Rich, eds. *Grand Strategy in the War Against Terrorism* (Portland: Frank Cass, 2003), 23.

[248] Byman, "Al-Qaeda as an Adversary," 162.

[249] Barry R. Posen, "The Struggle against Terrorism: Grand Strategy, Strategy, and Tactics," *International Security* 26, no. 3 (Winter 2001/02): 42-49.

[250] Ibid., 54.

potential threats, we will stretch ourselves to the breaking point and become more vulnerable – not less – to those truly in a position to harm us.[251]

To frame her proposed strategy, she continued, "The problem is not combating al Qaeda's inherent appeal, for it has none. The problem is changing the fact that major components of American foreign policy are either opposed or misunderstood by much of the world."[252] To address these perceptions, she suggested "a vastly expanded commitment to public diplomacy and outreach," and "a change in the tone of American national security policy to emphasize the value of diplomatic cooperation."[253] Continuing the same theme, while expressing the necessity of maintaining the global coalition formed in response to 9/11, Gunaratna called for "a concerted plan by the international community to redress the perceived and actual grievances of moderate Muslims," and public diplomacy efforts to discredit al Qaeda ideology.[254] He further emphasized the importance of setting the conditions in Afghanistan for a modern government to succeed. Finally, he warned against invasion of Iraq, as this would break up the global coalition while galvanizing support for al Qaeda.[255]

It has been previously demonstrated that the decision-making methodology of the administration facilitated a reluctance to pursue and consider outside advice and counsel, leading to a broad and myopic strategy heavily reliant on military power. As this section has demonstrated, this outside advice and counsel was abundant and available. If considered, the predominantly soft power-based approaches of the think tank and academic community may have influenced the administration toward adopting a less military-oriented strategy focused on countering the specific threat responsible for, and identified, on 9/11.

---

[251] Madeleine Albright, "Excerpts of Testimony from Madeleine Albright," in *The 9/11 Investigations*, ed. Steven Strasser (New York: PublicAffairs, 2004), 86.

[252] Ibid., 87.

[253] Ibid., 87.

[254] Rohan Gunaratna, *Inside al Qaeda: Global Network of Terror* (New York: Berkley Books, 2003), 315.

[255] Ibid., 315-318.

55

Positive Results

While broad and not focused on the immediate threat, bin Laden and al Qaeda, the initial strategy executed by the United States did result in a series of initial successes. In the first year following 9/11, the United States realized marked success and progress in targeting terrorist financing, arresting suspected terrorists, and degrading al Qaeda and the Taliban in Afghanistan. Further, the policy initiatives and programs across the whole of government led to continued success over the first decade following 9/11. In April, 2010, the Heritage Foundation identified thirty foiled terrorist plots against the United States. They asserted that twenty-eight of these successes were "the result of good law enforcement and effective intelligence gathering and information sharing."[256] The remaining two were owed to citizen involvement.[257] In a similar inquiry researching post-9/11 terrorist plots by Islamists against American civilians and military outside of designated war zones, John Avlon found, "The record shows that there have been at least 45 jihadist terrorist attacks plotted against Americans since 9/11—each of them thwarted by a combination of intelligence work, policing and citizen participation."[258]

The most quantifiable successes in the immediate aftermath of 9/11 were made in combating terrorist financing and arresting suspected terrorists. President Bush's Executive Order 13224 led to suspected terrorist assets and financing being frozen in "approximately 150 countries and independent law-enforcement jurisdictions."[259] In the first three months, the United States froze over thirty-four million dollars in terrorist assets, and an additional thirty-three

---

[256] Jena B. McNeill, James J. Carafano, and Jessica Zuckerman, "30 Terrorist Plots Foiled: How the System Works," The Heritage Foundation, http://www.heritage.org/research/reports/2010/04/30-terrorist-plots-foiled-how-the-system-worked (accessed January 30, 2012).

[257] Ibid.

[258] John Avlon, "Forty-Five Foiled Terror Plots Since 9/11," The Daily Beast, http://www.thedailybeast.com/articles/2011/09/08/9-11-anniversary-45-terror-plots-foiled-in-last-10-years.html (accessed January 30, 2012).

[259] U.S. Department of State, *Patterns of Global Terrorism* (Washington, DC, 2001), ix.

million dollars was blocked globally.[260] More specifically, the Department of the Treasury closed the al-Barakaat and al-Taqwa finance networks, effectively blocking twenty million dollars of al Qaeda assets. Both networks were directly related to al Qaeda and bin Laden, providing income, and funds transfer capabilities.[261] Global law enforcement, led by the FBI, was equally effective. Over 1,000 suspected terrorists were apprehended by law enforcement globally through May 2002.[262]

Parallel to these accomplishments, the military campaign in Afghanistan achieved remarkable success in its initial stages. Demonstrating global solidarity, 136 nations offered military assistance in the immediate aftermath of the attacks.[263] Within months, al Qaeda and the Taliban were effectively defeated, Hamid Karzai was leading the interim administration, and the process of nation-building in Afghanistan had begun. Following the rapid defeat of the Taliban, Bonn, Germany hosted a December, 2001 United Nations conference to outline a framework for the future governance of Afghanistan. The resultant agreement, known as the Bonn Agreement, established December 22, 2001 as the transfer date for the Interim Authority to be led by Karzai.[264] Coupled with the Bonn Agreement, the United Nations Security Council authorized the establishment of the International Security Assistance Force to provide a secure environment for the Interim Authority in Kabul.[265] Later, in March, 2002, the Security Council endorsed the establishment of the United Nations Assistance Mission in Afghanistan to manage the

---

[260] U.S. Department of State, *Patterns of Global Terrorism* (Washington, DC, 2001), x.

[261] Suskind, *The Price of Loyalty*, 198.

[262] U.S. Department of State, *Patterns of Global Terrorism* (Washington, DC, 2001), viii.

[263] Ibid., xii.

[264] United Nations, *Agreement on Provisional Arrangements in Afghanistan Pending the Re-establishment of Permanent Government Institutions*, December 5, 2001.

[265] United Nations Security Council, *Resolution 1386 on the Situation in Afghanistan*, December 20, 2001.

reconstruction effort.[266] In conjunction with these bureaucratic milestones, nearly two-thirds of al Qaeda's leadership were killed or captured.[267]

On the diplomatic front, the administration initially displayed indirect indications of addressing the 'why' of the attacks. On September 28, 2001, President Bush met with Jordan's King Abdullah at the White House.[268] White House Press Secretary Ari Fleischer recalled the President's comments that, "once Al Qaeda was dealt with, the United States would address the root causes of terror."[269] Fleischer then described "the parade of foreign leaders" who visited President Bush in the fall of 2001, recalling that, "invariably, the President would bring up the peace process between the Israelis and the Palestinians."[270]

The early actions of the administration produced numerous positive achievements. In his memoirs, President Bush reflected on his assessment of the executed strategy, "After the nightmare of September 11, America went seven and a half years without another successful terrorist attack on our soil. If I had to summarize my most meaningful accomplishment as President in one sentence, that would be it."[271]

Negative Implications

The initial success of America's response to 9/11 was soon overshadowed by the negative consequences resulting from the broad and unfocused strategy targeting objectives beyond bin Laden and al Qaeda. Referencing the wars in Iraq and Afghanistan, Condoleezza Rice

---

[266] United Nations Security Council, *Resolution 1401 on the Situation in Afghanistan*, March 28, 2002.

[267] Donald Rumsfeld, "Excerpts of Testimony from Donald Rumsfeld," in *The 9/11 Investigations*, ed. Steven Strasser (New York: PublicAffairs, 2004), 122.

[268] The White House: President George W. Bush, "King Abdullah of Jordan to Visit Washington," http://georgewbush-whitehouse.archives.gov/news/releases/2001/09/20010924-14.html (accessed December 27, 2011.

[269] Fleischer, *Taking Heat*, 186.

[270] Ibid., 208.

[271] Bush, *Decision Points*, 181.

testified before the 9/11 commission, "And as we attack the threat at its source, we are also addressing its roots."[272] This statement epitomized the misidentification and misunderstanding of our enemy. In his seminal work, *On War*, Clausewitz dictated that "War, therefore, is an act of policy."[273] He continued, "The political object is the goal, war is the means of reaching it, and means can never be considered in isolation from their purpose."[274] Bin Laden and al Qaeda's political objectives were clear. One month after 9/11, bin Laden reinforced them, stating, "America won't get out of this crisis until it gets out of the Arabian Peninsula, and until it stops its support of Israel."[275] By sending hundreds of thousands of troops to Iraq and Afghanistan, the United States did the exact opposite, contributing to the expansion of al Qaeda, and a reduction in the nation's comprehensive national power.

With its central command still operating from the Afghanistan-Pakistan region, al Qaeda has expanded to the Middle East and Africa since 9/11, and has continued to prosecute its global terror campaign. In 2005, Bruce Hoffman testified to Congress, "For al Qaeda, accordingly, Iraq has likely been a very useful side-show: an effective means to preoccupy American military forces and distract U.S. attention while al Qaeda and its confederates make new inroads and strike elsewhere."[276] Supporting Hoffman's prediction, Al Qaeda affiliates now include Al Qaeda in the Arabian Peninsula, Al Qaeda in the Islamic Maghreb, and Al Qaeda-linked al-Shabab in

---

[272] Condoleezza Rice, "Excerpts of Testimony from Condoleezza Rice," in *The 9/11 Investigations*, ed. Steven Strasser (New York: PublicAffairs, 2004), 217-218.

[273] Carl von Clausewitz, *On War*, trans. and ed. Michael Howard and Peter Paret (Princeton, NJ: Princeton University Press, 1984), 86-87.

[274] Ibid., 87.

[275] Osama bin Laden, interview by Tayseer Alouni, Afghanistan, October 21, 2001, transcript, http://articles.cnn.com/2002-02-05/world/binladen.transcript_1_incitement-fatwas-al-qaeda-organization?_s=PM:asiapcf (accessed February 2, 2012).

[276] Bruce Hoffman, "Does Our Counter-Terrorism Strategy Match the Threat?" (testimony presented before the House International Relations Committee, Subcommittee on International Terrorism and Nonproliferation, Washington DC, September 29, 2005).

Somalia.[277] Further, al Qaeda in Iraq has indicated signs of resurgence with the recent withdrawal

of American troops.[278] Previously focused regionally, these affiliates have transformed to a more

global focus under the al Qaeda banner.[279] Demonstrating al Qaeda's continued capability,

Microsoft National Broadcasting Company compiled a summary of al Qaeda executed and

motivated attacks in the four years following 9/11, which included twenty-three successful

attacks, outside of designated war zones, resulting in 925 deaths.[280] More recently, al Qaeda has

been responsible for the 2008 bombing of the U.S. Embassy in Yemen,[281] the 2009 attempted

attack on Northwest Flight 253,[282] and the 2010 plot to bomb cargo aircraft bound for the United

States.[283]

In conjunction with the undisciplined terrorism strategy's failure to contain al Qaeda, it

contributed to the degradation of the United States' diplomatic and economic elements of national

power. Director Tenet affirmed the imperative of cultivating and maintaining a coalition to

respond to 9/11, stating, "There is one important moral to the story: you cannot fight terrorism

alone. There were clear limitations to what we could do without the help of like-minded

---

[277] Sudarsan Raghavan and Craig Whitlock, "Al-Qaeda Affiliates Poised to Produce New Leaders," *The Washington Post*, http://www.washingtonpost.com/world/following-bin-ladens-death-al-qaeda-affiliates-in-africa-middle-east-poised-to-produce-new-leaders/2011/05/02/AFaJIwYF_story.html (accessed January 31, 2012).

[278] "Al Qaeda in Iraq Claims Responsibility for Recent Attacks," CNN, http://www.cnn.com/2011/12/27/world/meast/iraq-violence/index.html (accessed February 1, 2012).

[279] Daniel L. Byman, "Al Qaeda's M&A Strategy," The Brookings Institute, http://www.brookings.edu/opinions/2010/1207_al_qaeda_byman.aspx (accessed January 31, 2012).

[280] Robert Windrem, "Al-Qaida Timeline: Plots and Attacks," MSNBC, http://www.msnbc msn.com/id/4677978/ns/world_news-hunt_for_al_qaida/t/al-qaida-timeline-plots-attacks/ (accessed January 31, 2012).

[281] "Blasts Rock US Embassy in Yemen," BBC, http://news.bbc.co.uk/2/hi/middle_east/7620362.stm (accessed February 1, 2012).

[282] Richard Esposito and Brian Ross, "Photos of the Northwest Airlines Flight 253 Bomb," ABC News, http://abcnews.go.com/Blotter/northwest-airlines-flight-253-bomb-photos-exclusive/story?id=9436297 (accessed February 1, 2012).

[283] Jamie Doward and Mark Townsend, "Terror Bombs Were Primed to Down Cargo Planes in Mid-Air," The Guardian, http://www.guardian.co.uk/world/2010/oct/30/cargo-plane-bombs-explode-midair (accessed February 1, 2012).

governments."[284] The expansion of the strategy beyond bin Laden and al Qaeda jeopardized this pursuit. Richard Haass, President of the Council on Foreign Relations, suggested, "Diplomatically, this war has contributed to the world's alienation from the United States."[285] Similarly, Andrew Tan argued that, in the eyes of the global community, the United States squandered "its soft power and legitimacy. This has come about through the Bush administration's unilateral, military-oriented approach and controversial actions, such as the invasion of Iraq."[286]

Specific to addressing the long-term problem of radical Islamic terrorism, the United States' foreign policy following 9/11 contributed to widespread negative perceptions in the Islamic world. A 2007 Program on International Policy Attitudes analysis found that seventy-five percent of the Islamic world held an unfavorable view of the U.S. government. Further, their research found that seventy-four percent approved of getting U.S. military forces to withdraw from Islamic countries.[287] In 2011, Steven Kull, who participated in the 2007 project, concluded a related five-year study of Muslim feelings toward America. He concluded that "throughout the Middle East and South Asia, hostility toward the United States persists unabated." These sentiments contribute to an environment favorable to terrorist recruiting, funding, and operations free from government interference.[288]

---

[284] Tenet, *At the Center of the Storm*, 129.

[285] Richard N. Haass, interview by Bernard Gwertzman, March 14, 2006, transcript, http://www.cfr.org/iraq/haass-balance-iraq-wars-impact-us-foreign-policy-clearly-negative/p10132 (accessed January 31, 2012).

[286] Andrew T. H. Tan, *U.S. Strategy Against Global Terrorism: How It Evolved, Why It Failed, and Where It is Headed* (New York: Palgrave Macmillan, 2009), 13.

[287] Steven Kull, "Negative Attitudes toward the United States in the Muslim World: Do They Matter?" (testimony presented before the House Foreign Affairs Committee, Subcommittee on International Organizations, Human Rights, and Oversight, Washington DC, May 17, 2007).

[288] Steven Kull, "Why Muslims are Still Mad at America," World Public Opinion.org, http://www.worldpublicopinion.org/pipa/articles/brmiddleeastnafricara/691.php?lb=brme&pnt=691&nid=&id= (accessed January 31, 2012).

Similarly, the military campaigns had a profound impact on the economic strength of the United States. In an email to Taliban leader Mullah Omar on October 3, 2001 bin Laden stated, "A campaign against Afghanistan will impose great long-term economic burdens, leading to further economic collapse, which will force America, God willing, to resort to the former Soviet Union's only option: withdrawal from Afghanistan, disintegration, and contraction."[289] The campaign in Afghanistan, coupled with the Iraq war, did perpetuate significant economic burdens. In the decade following fiscal year 2001, the U.S. public debt grew from 3.3 trillion dollars to 10.1 trillion dollars.[290] More importantly, the nation's public debt to gross domestic product ratio doubled from thirty-two percent to sixty-six percent over the same period, and continues to rise representing significant vulnerability of the U.S. economy.[291]

The Congressional Research Service estimated the total direct cost of the Global War on Terror through the end of fiscal year 2012 to be 1.4 trillion dollars. Using Congressional Budget Office projections, the total cost could increase to 1.8 trillion dollars by 2021.[292] Incorporating related current and future expenses, a June 2011 study by Brown University's Eisenhower Research Project estimated the total costs of the War on Terror to be between 3.2 and 4 trillion dollars.[293] This figure would represent approximately half of the public debt expansion over the past decade. In addition to the direct costs of the wars, Harvard Professor Linda Bilmes and Nobel Laureate Joseph Stiglitz contend that the war in Iraq shaped the conditions that led to the

---

[289] Alan Cullison, "Inside Al-Qaeda's Hard Drive," *The Atlantic*, September, 2004.

[290] "The Debt to the Penny and Who Holds It," U.S. Department of the Treasury, Bureau of the Public Debt, http://www.treasurydirect.gov/NP/BPDLogin?application=np (accessed January 31, 2012).

[291] "National Income and Products Account Table," U.S. Department of Commerce, http://www.bea.gov/national/nipaweb/TableView.asp?SelectedTable=5&FirstYear=2010&LastYear=2011&Freq=Qtr (accessed January 31, 2012).

[292] Congressional Research Service, *The Cost of Iraq, Afghanistan, and Other Global War on Terror Operations Since 9/11*, Amy Belasco (Washington DC, 2011).

[293] "Estimated Cost of Post-9/11 Wars: 225,000 Lives, up to $4 Trillion," Brown University, http://news.brown.edu/pressreleases/2011/06/warcosts, and http://costsofwar.org/article/economic-cost-summary (accessed January 31, 2012).

nation's 2008 financial crisis. The instability in the region created by the war contributed to the escalation in oil prices from thirty dollars per barrel in 2003 to 140 dollars per barrel in 2008. These "Higher oil prices threatened to depress U.S. economic activity, prompting the Federal Reserve to lower interest rates and loosen regulations. These policies were major contributors to the housing bubble and the financial collapse that followed."[294] Culminating the nation's vulnerability, Standard and Poor, for the first time in its history, downgraded the United States' credit rating from AAA to AA+ on August 5, 2011.[295]

By pursuing an overreaching strategy that extended beyond the threat posed on 9/11, the comprehensive national power of the United States has been reduced. In not properly identifying the enemy, or their motives, the administration embarked on a strategy that failed to eliminate the threat, and subsequently reduced the diplomatic and economic standing of the nation.

Conclusion

This monograph emphasized the necessity of properly identifying and focusing on the enemy. The enemy presented on 9/11 was Osama bin Laden and al Qaeda, not terrorism. Terrorism is a tactic, not a person or an organization, that has been and will continue to be used as a mechanism to achieve political ends. Prior to 9/11, Sandia National Laboratory's 1999 case study emphasized this point, stating, "The 'war' against terrorism will never be 'won': terrorism will always be a world problem."[296] The same is true today.

After identifying the enemy, the corresponding imperative is to understand the enemy. Bin Laden's declared war against America was motivated by U.S. foreign policy and presence in

---

[294] Linda J. Bilmes and Joseph E. Stiglitz, "America's Costly War Machine: Fighting the War on Terror Compromises the Economy Now and Threatens it in the Future," *Los Angeles Times*, http://articles.latimes.com/2011/sep/18/opinion/la-oe--bilmes-war-cost-20110918 (accessed January 31, 2012).

[295] Zachary A. Goldfarb, "S&P Downgrades U.S. Credit Rating for First Time," *The Washington Post*, http://www.washingtonpost.com/business/economy/sandp-considering-first-downgrade-of-us-credit-rating/2011/08/05/gIQAqKeIxI_story.html (accessed January 31, 2012).

[296] Sandia National Laboratories, *Osama bin Laden: A Case Study*, 5.

the Middle East. In his 1998 interview with John Miller, he demanded, "My word to American journalists is not to ask why we did that, but to ask what had their government done that forced us to defend ourselves?"[297] Speaking directly to U.S. presence in the Middle East, he proclaimed "that every day the Americans delay their departure, for every day they delay, they will receive a new corpse from Muslim countries."[298] The deployment of hundreds of thousands of U.S. troops to Muslim countries over the past decade serves to indicate the American misunderstanding of the threat by antagonizing the very focal point of bin Laden's and al Qaeda's grievances.

Director Tenet and General Myers encapsulated these points in their retrospective memoirs. Director Tenet, referencing the expansion of the strategy's execution to include Iraq questioned, "What never happened, as far as I can tell, was a serious consideration of the implications of a U.S. invasion. What impact would a large American occupying force have in an Arab country in the heart of the Middle East?"[299] General Myers offered similar sentiments, stating, "We have failed to adequately define our adversary and, therefore, lack an appropriate strategy for dealing with that adversary."[300]

A decade later, this failure to accurately define the enemy has manifested itself in the inability to defeat or contain al Qaeda, and the undermining of the United States' comprehensive national power, specifically diplomatic influence and economic might. History is studied to learn and understand in order to be better leaders, and to apply past lessons to present and future problems. The lessons of the United States' 9/11 response are profound, and should be studied by today's and tomorrow's leaders in order to inform strategy development and decision-making in meeting tomorrow's national security challenges.

---

[297] Osama bin Laden, interview by John Miller, May 28, 1998, Afghanistan, transcript, http://www.freerepublic.com/focus/news/833647/posts (accessed August 29, 2011).

[298] Ibid.

[299] Tenet, *At the Center of the Storm*, 308.

[300] Myers, *Eyes on the Horizon*, 284.

BIBLIOGRAPHY

Primary Sources

Atwan, Abdel Bari. *The Secret History of al Qaeda*. Berkeley, CA: University of California Press, 2006.

Bennett, Gina. *The Wandering Mujahidin: Armed and Dangerous*. Washington DC: U.S. Department of State Bureau of Intelligence and Research, August 21-22, 1993. http://www.nationalsecuritymom.com/3/WanderingMujahidin.pdf (accessed December 9, 2011).

Bush, George W. *Decision Points*. New York: Crown Publishers, 2010.

Cheney, Richard B. *In My Time: A Personal and Political Memoir*. New York: Threshold Editions, 2011.

Clarke, Richard A. *Against All Enemies: Inside America's War on Terror*. New York: Free Press, 2004.

Feith, Douglas J. *War and Decision: Inside the Pentagon at the Dawn of the War on Terrorism*. New York: HarperCollins, 2008.

Fisk, Robert. "Osama bin Laden: The Godfather of Terror." *The Independent*, September 15, 2001. http://www.independent.co.uk/news/people/profiles/osama-bin-laden-the-godfather-of-terror-751944.html (accessed August 25, 2011).

Fleischer, Ari. *Taking Heat: The President, the Press, and My Years in the White House*. New York: HarperCollins, 2005.

Franks, Tommy. *American Soldier*. New York: ReganBooks, 2004.

Frum, David. *The Right Man: The Surprise Presidency of George W. Bush*. New York: Random House, 2003.

Fury, Dalton. *Kill Bin Laden: A Delta Force Commander's Account of the Hunt for the World's Most Wanted Man*. New York: St. Martin's Griffin, 2008.

Kepel, Gilles, and Jean-Pierre Milelli, eds. *Al Qaeda in its Own Words*. Translated by Pascale Ghazaleh. Cambridge, MA: The Belknap Press of Harvard University Press, 2008.

Kull, Steven. "Negative Attitudes toward the United States in the Muslim World: Do They Matter?" Testimony presented before the House Foreign Affairs Committee, Subcommittee on International Organizations, Human Rights, and Oversight, Washington DC, May 17, 2007.

Mueller, Robert S. III. "The FBI Transformation Since 2001." Remarks before the House Appropriations Subcommittee on Science, the Departments of State, Justice and Commerce, and Related Agencies, Washington DC, September 14, 2001.

Myers, Richard B., and Malcolm McConnell. *Eyes on the Horizon: Serving on the Front Lines of National Security*. New York: Threshold Editions, 2009.

National Commission on Terrorist Attacks upon the United States. *The 9/11 Commission Report*. New York: W.W. Norton & Company, 2004.

National Review, ed. *"We Will Prevail": President George W. Bush on War, Terrorism, and Freedom*. New York: Continuum, 2003.

Osama bin Laden. interview by Al Jazeera. Afghanistan, 1998. transcript, http://www.freerepublic.com/focus/f-news/542192/posts (accessed August 25, 2011).

Osama bin Laden. interview by Tayseer Alouni. Afghanistan, October 21, 2001. transcript, http://articles.cnn.com/2002-02-05/world/binladen.transcript_1_incitement-fatwas-al-qaeda-organization?_s=PM:asiapcf (accessed February 2, 2012).

Osama bin Laden. interview by Peter Arnett. Afghanistan, March 1997. transcript, http://fl1.findlaw.com/news.findlaw.com/cnn/docs/binladen/binladenintvw-cnn.pdf (accessed February 2, 2012).

Osama bin Laden. interview by John Miller. Afghanistan, May 28, 1998. transcript, http://www.pbs.org/wgbh/pages/frontline/shows/binladen/who/interview.html (accessed August 25, 2011).

Osama bin Laden. interview by Rahimullah Yusufzai. Afghanistan, December 23, 1998. transcript, http://www.time.com/time/world/article/0,8599,2054517,00.html (accessed August 25, 2011).

Rice, Condoleezza. *No Higher Honor: A Memoir of My Years in Washington*. New York: Crown Publishers, 2011.

Rove, Karl. *Courage and Consequences: My Life as a Conservative in the Fight*. New York: Threshold Editions, 2010.

Rumsfeld, Donald. *Known and Unknown: A Memoir*. New York: Sentinel, 2011.

Strasser, Steven, ed. *The 9/11 Investigations*. New York: Public Affairs, 2004.

Suskind, Ron. *The Price of Loyalty: George W. Bush, the White House, and the Education of Paul O'Neill*. New York: Simon & Schuster, 2004.

Tenet, George. *At the Center of the Storm: My Years at the CIA*. New York: HarperCollins, 2007.

U.S. Department of State. *Patterns of Global Terrorism: 1998*. Washington DC: April, 1999.

U.S. Department of State. *Patterns of Global terrorism: 1999*. Washington DC: April, 2000.

U.S. Department of State. *Patterns of Global terrorism: 2000*. Washington DC: April, 2001.

U.S. Department of State. *Patterns of Global terrorism: 2001*. Washington DC: May, 2002.

U.S. President. *National Security Strategy of the United States of America*. September, 2002.

U.S. President. *National Strategy for Combating Terrorism*. February, 2003.

U.S. President. *National Strategy for Homeland Security*. July, 2002.

Secondary Sources

Byman, Daniel L. "Al-Qaeda as an Adversary: Do We Understand Our Enemy?" *World Politics* 56 (October 2003): 139-163.

Cordesman, Anthony H., and Arleigh A. Burke, *A New US Strategy for Counter-Terrorism and Asymmetric Warfare*. Washington DC: Center for Strategic and International Studies, 2001.

Cronin, Audrey K. "How al-Qaida Ends: The Decline and Demise of Terrorist Groups." *International Security* 31, no. 1 (Summer 2006): 7-48.

Davis, Lynn E., and Melanie W. Sisson. *A Strategic Planning Approach: Defining Alternative Counterterrorism Strategies as an Illustration*, Occasional Paper. Santa Monica, CA: RAND Corporation, 2009.

Falkenrath, Richard A. "Grading the War on Terrorism." *Foreign Affairs* 85, no. 1 (Jan/Feb 2006): 122-128.

Farrall, Leah. "How Al Qaeda Works: What the Organization's Subsidiaries Say About Its Strength." *Foreign Affairs* 90, no. 2 (Mar/Apr 2011): 128-138.

"Fighting Terrorism with Democracy: A Losing Strategy." Paper presented at the Global International Studies Conference, Istanbul, Turkey, August 24, 2005.

Hoffman, Bruce. "Combating Terrorism: In Search of a National Strategy." Testimony presented before the House Committee on Government Reform, Subcommittee on National Security, Veterans Affairs, and International Relations, Washington DC, March 27, 2001.

Hoffman, Bruce. "Does Our Counter-Terrorism Strategy Match the Threat?" Testimony presented before the House International Relations Committee, Subcommittee on International Terrorism and Nonproliferation, Washington DC, September 29, 2005.

Hoffman, Bruce. "Lessons of 9/11." Submitted for the Committee Record to the United States Joint September 11, 2001 Inquiry Staff of the House and Senate Select Committees on Intelligence, Washington DC, October 8, 2002.

Hoffman, Bruce. "Preparing for the War on Terrorism." Testimony presented before the House Committee on Government Reform, Subcommittee on National Security, Veterans Affairs, and International Relations, Washington DC, September, 2001.

Hoffman, Bruce. "Re-thinking Terrorism in Light of a War on Terrorism." Testimony presented before the House Permanent Select Committee on Intelligence, Subcommittee on Terrorism and Homeland Security, Washington DC, September 26, 2001.

Jenkins, Brian M. "Remarks before the National Commission on Terrorist Attacks Upon the United States." Testimony presented to the National Commission on Terrorist Attacks Upon the United States, Washington DC, March 31, 2003.

Parachini, John V. "The 9/11 Commission Recommendations and the National Strategies." Testimony presented to the House Committee of Government Reform, Subcommittee on National Security, Emerging Threats, and International Relations, Washington D.C., September 22, 2004.

Posen, Barry R. "The Struggle against Terrorism: Grand Strategy, Strategy, and Tactics." *International Security* 26, no. 3 (Winter 2001/02): 39-55.

Sandia National Laboratories. *Osama bin Laden: A Case Study*. Livermore, CA: December 1999. http://www.gwu.edu/~nsarchiv/NSAEBB/NSAEBB343/osama_bin_laden_file04.pdf (accessed December 5, 2011).

Schwenninger, Sherle R. "Revamping American Grand Strategy." *World Policy Journal* 20, no. 3 (Fall 2003): 25-44.

U.S. Congress. House. Committee on International Relations. *Hearing on Al Qaeda and the Global Reach of Terrorism*. 107th Cong., 1st sess., October 3, 2001.

Books

Beitler, Ruth Margolies. "The Complex Relationship between Global Terrorism and U.S. Support for Israel." in *The Making of a Terrorist: Recruitment, Training, and Root Causes*, vol 3, edited by James J.F. Forest, 62-73. Westport, Connecticut: Praeger Security International, 2006.

Benjamin, Daniel, and Steven Simon. *The Next Attack: The Failure of the War on Terror and a Strategy for Getting it Right*. New York: Times Books, 2005.

Bergen, Peter L. *Holy War, Inc.: Inside the Secret World of Osama Bin Laden*. New York: Simon & Schuster, 2002.

Bergen, Peter L. *The Longest War: The Enduring Conflict Between America and Al-Qaeda*. New York: Free Press, 2011.

Burke, Jason. *Al Qaeda: Casting a Shadow of Terror*. New York: I.B. Tauris, 2003.

Clarke, Richard A., Glenn P. Aga, Roger W. Cressey, Stephen E. Flynn, Blake W. Mobley, Eric Rosenbach, Steven Simon, William F. Wechsler, and Lee S. Wolosky. *Defeating the Jihadists: A Blueprint for Action*. New York: Century Foundation, 2004.

Clarke, Richard A. *Your Government Failed You: Breaking the Cycle of National Security Disasters*. New York: HarperCollins, 2008.

Esposito, Alice F., ed. *Al Qaeda: Background, Evolution and Assessment*. New York: Nova Science Publishers, 2010.

Frum, David, and Richard Perle. *An End to Evil: How to Win the War on Terror*. New York: Ballantine Books, 2004.

Greenberg, Karen J., ed. *Al Qaeda Now: Understanding Today's Terrorists*. New York: Cambridge University Press, 2005.

Gunaratna, Rohan. *Inside Al Qaeda: Global Network of Terror*. New York: Berkley Books, 2003.

Herspring, Dale R. *The Pentagon and the Presidency: Civil-Military Relations from FDR to George W. Bush*. Lawrence, Kansas: University Press of Kansas, 2005.

Hess, Gary R. *Presidential Decisions for War: Korea, Vietnam, the Persian Gulf, and Iraq*. 2nd ed. Baltimore: The Johns Hopkins University Press, 2009.

Kull, Steven. *Feeling Betrayed: The Roots of Muslim Anger at America*. Washington DC: Brookings Institute Press, 2011.

Mockaitis, Thomas R., and Paul B. Rich, eds. *Grand Strategy in the War Against Terrorism*. Portland: Frank Cass, 2003.

Mohammad, Abdullah Yousef Sahar. "Roots of Terrorism in the Middle East: Internal Pressures and International Constraints." in *Root Causes of Terrorism: Myths, Reality, and Ways Forward*, edited by Tore Bjørgo, 103-118. New York: Routledge, 2006.

Pape, Robert A. *Dying to Win: The Strategic Logic of Suicide Terrorism*. New York: Random House, 2005.

Pollock, Kenneth M. *The Threatening Storm: The Case for Invading Iraq*. New York: Random House, 2002.

Richardson, Louise. *What Terrorists Want*. New York: Random House, 2006.

Riedel, Bruce. *The Search for Al Qaeda: Its Leadership, Ideology, and Future*. Washington DC: Brookings Institute Press, 2008.

Sageman, Marc. *Understanding Terror Networks*. Philadelphia: University of Pennsylvania Press, 2004.

Scheuer, Michael. *Through Our Enemies' Eyes: Osama bin Laden, Radical Islam, and the Future of America*. 2nd ed. Washington DC: Potomac Books, 2006.

Schmid, Alex P., and Ronald D. Crelinsten, eds. *Western Responses to Terrorism*. London, England: Frank Cass, 1993.

Tan, Andrew T. H. *U.S. Strategy Against Global Terrorism: How It Evolved, Why It Failed, and Where It is Headed*. New York: Palgrave Macmillan, 2009.

Turabian, Kate L. *A Manual for Writers of Research Papers, Theses, and Dissertations*. 7th ed. Chicago: University of Chicago Press, 2007.

Woodward, Bob. *Bush at War*. New York: Simon & Schuster, 2002.